# MISREADING
# MASCULINITY

# MISREADING MASCULINITY

## Boys, Literacy, and Popular Culture

Thomas Newkirk

University of New Hampshire

*Foreword by Ellin Oliver Keene*

HEINEMANN

PORTSMOUTH, NH

Heinemann

361 Hanover Street
Portsmouth, NH 03801–3912
www.heinemann.com

*Offices and agents throughout the world*

The author and publisher wish to thank those who have generously given permission to reprint borrowed material:

The Jim Borgman editorial cartoon (6/6/99) that appears in Chapter 1 is reprinted by special permission of King Features Syndicate.

Figures 2–1 and 2–2 are reprinted from *The ETS Gender Study: How Females and Males Perform in Educational Settings,* May 1997. Reprinted by permission of Educational Testing Service, the copyright owner.

**Library of Congress Cataloging-in-Publication Data**
Newkirk, Thomas.
    Misreading masculinity : boys, literacy, and popular culture / Thomas Newkirk.
        p. cm.
    Includes bibliographical references.
    ISBN 0-325-00445-5
    1. Boys—Education (Elementary)—Social aspects—United States.
2. Language arts (Elementary)—Social aspects—United States.
3. Masculinity in popular culture—United States. 4. Violence in popular culture—United States. I. Title.

LC1396.4 .N49 2002
371.823—dc21                                                          2002004351


Editors: Leigh Peake and Alan Huisman
Production: Vicki Kasabian
Interior and cover design: Jenny Jensen Greenleaf
Cover photograph: W. Garrett Scholes
Typesetter: Argosy
Manufacturing: Steve Bernier

Printed in the United States of America on acid-free paper
11 10 09          VP          8 9 10

*To Maurice Newkirk*
1914–2001

# CONTENTS

Occasionally you read an article or an op/ed piece that shakes the foundation of your most strongly held beliefs and assumptions. You generally begin with some skepticism; perhaps the writer is someone with whom you have disagreed in the past. You may be aware that his or her political views are usually quite different from your own and you resolve to give this poor schmuck no more than his first paragraph to dissuade you of your dearly held beliefs. Usually, he doesn't and, comfortable and smug in your inherent rightness, you go on to read the column written by your political hero who is, as usual, brilliantly on point and scathing in his criticism of the politician you love to hate. It feels good.

But once in a long, long while you read the enemy's first paragraph and something involuntarily flashes through your mind. The guy has a point. Surely that couldn't be right. You repress the thought but keep reading. His argument builds logically and you fight the annoying voice in your mind that is agreeing with this writer. None of it fits with the devastatingly insightful arguments you made last evening at a party when you were engaged in verbal battle with your spouse's boss who everyone knows is a fool. Ah, but as you read you must admit that this guy has a point. By the end of the piece, you realize that, to be intellectually honest, you have to reconsider your heretofore passionately held notion of the irreversible truth. The guy has a point.

Now, Tom Newkirk is anything but a mortal political enemy with whom I routinely disagree. He is a colleague, my editor, and a dear friend. In our dozens of conversations through the years, I have nearly always not only agreed but admired his arguments and the thoughtful way he presents them. As I began to read *Misreading Masculinity*, however, I found myself really wondering. Could Tom possibly be suggesting that it may not always be right to "write what you know"? Could he really be challenging conventional wisdom about imposing restrictions on children's writing that depicts violence or disgusting bodily sounds? Does he really want to read that stuff? At first, I argued with him in my mind. Then, my acceptance of the conventional wisdom began to waver.

In *Misreading Masculinity*, Tom Newkirk challenges the standards and the standard bearers in literacy on behalf of boys. In a captivating set of arguments brilliantly unwound across the chapters of this book, Tom wages his own (nonviolent) battle with the assumptions I and thousands of other literacy educators have long held when it comes to the topics and genres some children, particularly boys, choose to write and read.

The more I read of this book, the more I found myself nodding in bemused agreement. I wondered how many times I have said no to a young writer who wished to use action, adventure, and excitement to immerse himself in another world or, as Tom suggests, even *improve* his present circumstances through his adventure writing. I wondered how many times I've said "write what you know" and looked forward to a touching personal narrative that predicted how socially conscious a child would be as an adult. I called that topic choice?!? I began to recall the numerous occasions when I had suggested that a young man reserve a comic book or horror novel for "at home" reading. I called that book choice?!?

*Misreading Masculinity* will recall to the reader's conscious mind the lurking questions and qualms he or she has had about the inherent rightness of certain assumptions made in literacy classrooms. For example, are television plots ever a legitimate narrative for classroom discussion? Tom suggests that, unwittingly, educators may have created an intellectual elitism that excludes too many children—perhaps as many as 50 percent—the boys and young men in our K–12 classrooms. In a series of fascinating interviews with both girls and boys, Tom shows us that the insights and understandings boys extract from popular culture may be profound, though they come from what many educators consider illegitimate sources. Can Bart Simpson shed light on the meaning of life? According to Tom's interviewees, he can indeed.

More to the point, the boys in this book make clear their ability to distinguish fantasy from reality and their sense of a need for moderation in writing about blood and gore in their fiction. *Misreading Masculinity* challenges us to **give kids credit**—it shows that they can understand the dangers in the world around them and that the vast majority can cognitively manage violence in the books they read and use it sparingly in their writing.

To read *Misreading Masculinity* is to be reminded of the elegance of an argument brilliantly constructed, supported with research, and supplemented with insights from masterful thinkers across history. But to read *Misreading Masculinity* is also a journey with the author through his own schooling and his experiences raising two girls and a boy, Andy, his youngest. Tom invokes Rousseau and Montaigne to remind us of the power of physical learning but also weaves in stories of his own squirmy fourth-grade self vastly relieved by a teacher who invites him to take a little walk outside. We also howl with laughter as Tom views the movie *Dumb and Dumber* with his son, a friend, and the mother of the friend, a virtual stranger about whom Tom has serious questions regarding her willingness to laugh her way through the farts and burps offered up by the movie.

We are introduced to Jamie, who is the type of child we have all been conditioned to worry about but who Tom shows to be insightful, able to visualize with extraordinary detail and sustain writing on a single piece for a long period of time. Tom shows, through an analysis of Jamie's writing, that the great themes of classic literature—good versus evil, hero versus underdog, and many others—are alive and well in Jamie's work.

As I put this book down, I marveled at Tom's ability to marry the worlds of the scholar and practitioner. How many books, currently available, speak so directly to both audiences? *Misreading Masculinity* is exactly the kind of book serious researchers should read. They will be gratified by the logic, the clarity, and the strength of Tom's arguments, the solid base of research on which those arguments rest. But *Misreading Masculinity* is especially the kind of book practitioners should read. In it they will find that their assumptions and beliefs are challenged in a way that can only improve their interactions with children, not to mention their own intellectual reasoning. They will be reminded of the grace of a well-constructed argument and will be deeply grateful to Tom for sprinkling his great humor through these pages as he systematically asks us to rethink our beliefs, our choices, our interactions—not just with boys but with all children.

*Ellin Oliver Keene*

# ACKNOWLEDGMENTS

This book is the product of many great conversations, some with colleagues and editors, but many with fathers and mothers puzzled by the reluctance of their sons to read and write. Often they would pull out something written at home—a jokebook or comic strip, a space story or labeled drawings of weapons—to suggest that their sons were literate, but not in the way schools promoted or rewarded. I think their interest in my project, their sense of its relevance, convinced me that this was not simply an academic pursuit. I hope this book offers them something in return.

I am indebted to Bob Connors, who opened up questions of masculinity and literacy in the early 1990s—and took a good deal of criticism for it. His death in 2000 was a personal loss to all of us at the University of New Hampshire and to a wide circle of admirers in the field of composition. It deprived me of many good late-afternoon conversations in the great clutter of his office.

Lad Tobin patiently listened to many of the ideas in this book on our hikes in the White Mountains, and when the manuscript was finished he gave it an extraordinarily helpful close reading. His own writing remains for me a model of what scholarship can be—probing, grounded in the realities of teaching, and engaging to read.

I had the cooperation of several area teachers, Ann Zwart, David McCormick, Barbara Page, Sue Tozier, and Mike Anderson. Their willingness to open their classrooms to me is deeply appreciated.

Of course my debt to the children themselves is immense. Jack Wilde, as always, helped me think through much of this; his uncanny ability to find *my* wavelength has been a lasting gift for me.

At the University of New Hampshire, I benefited from conversations with Cindy Gannett, Paula Salvio, Michael Brosnan, and John Lofty. Cindy's work on gendered literacy traditions was surely an early seed of this project. Thanks also to the Learning Through Teaching consultants: Pat McLure, Jean Robbins, Rita Georgeou, Phil Yeaton, Tomasen Carey, Emma Rous, Betty Sprague, and Pam Mueller. Louise Wrobleski took a keen interest in this project, bringing in a number of significant writing samples. I am also grateful to the university's English department and college of liberal arts for a course reduction that gave me needed time to write.

My debts to scholars is the field are, of course, too numerous to mention here. That's what bibliographies are for. But I do want to single out Michael Smith and Jeff Wilhelm, whose excellent book *"Reading Don't Fix No Chevys": The Role of Literacy in the Lives of Young Men* I read in manuscript as I was finishing my own. I also want to acknowledge my appreciation of Anne Haas Dyson, whose footprints (or is it fingerprints?) are all over this work. Finally, Joseph Tobin's *"Good Guys Don't Wear Hats": Children's Talk About the Media* established for me the complexity of children's engagement with visual media. I admire the way he stirs things up.

At Heinemann, I want to thank Maura Sullivan, who gave me a kick in the pants that helped me get started writing. I enjoyed early conversations and encouragement from Bill Varner, whom I will miss at 361 Hanover Street. Alan Huisman, Heinemann super-editor, gave the manuscript an encouraging and helpful reading. Special thanks to Leigh Peake, who brought to this project, as to so many others, just the right blend of enthusiasm and critical rigor. She never makes it seem like work. And thanks to Shannon Goff for her careful proofreading.

A final thanks to my family, Beth, Sarah, Abby, and Andy, for their support and for tolerating the loud symphonic music in my study (essential to the writing process). A special thanks to my son, Andy, who was finally able to demonstrate to my satisfaction that it *is possible* to recite the entire alphabet in a single burp.

# The Believing Game

I am an American, Chicago-born—Chicago, that somber city—and go at things as I have taught myself, freestyle, and will make the record in my own way: first to knock, first admitted....

—Opening to *The Adventures of Augie March*, by Saul Bellow

This book will be part memoir, part guide to teaching boys, part research project, part cultural analysis, part review of published research. It is written "freestyle" in a mixture of genres. At times in the writing I have imagined myself as a defense attorney making the case for the "low status" narratives enjoyed by boys—comics, jokes, media games, plot-driven fiction, sports tables. I hope to encourage those in schools to ask questions about what counts as literacy and what doesn't.

I am not using "literacy" in the loose way it has come to be employed—as virtually any competence. After all, if we can have "environmental literacy," "visual literacy," and "mechanical literacy," why not "gardening literacy" or "cooking literacy" (or "sexual literacy")? I am primarily interested in the *written* stories children choose to read and compose, although these stories often involve illustration, and they are often drawn from cinematic models. My primary focus will be on the later elementary grades because the stories at this age are often so elaborate, so very *un-adultlike*. As one third grader put it, "In fiction, you make your own personal world, your own world, your own rules." This book is an attempt to understand these rules.

In many ways the writing of both younger and older students made more sense to me. Who could not appreciate the literacy breakthroughs of primary students, the miraculous invented spelling, and the astonishing growth? In middle school and beyond, students seem more adept at and interested in the kind of realism that we as adult readers enjoy. But the writing of older elementary students often seemed to me extravagantly different, a special genre, or set of genres, that includes friends, quotations from popular culture, and plots that don't quit—sequel after sequel. This writing often exhausted me, confused me. How could these young writers enjoy this writing that gave me so little pleasure as a reader? The task I set for myself was to play what Peter Elbow (1973) calls "the believing game," to read this work generously, to capture the intention and pleasure of the young writers, particularly the boys. As a general rule, no one voluntarily persists at work they find meaningless—so what is the meaning, the payoff, for these endlessly repeated space stories?

But more is at stake here than a personal curiosity about boys' writing in the upper elementary grades. I will argue that too many of our schools are failing too many of our boys, particularly in the area of reading and writing. By defining, teaching, and evaluating literacy in narrow ways—even under the banner of "choice" and a student-centered curriculum—we have failed to support, or even allow, in our literacy programs the tastes, values, and learning styles of many boys. More specifically, we have discouraged, devalued, or even prohibited the genres of reading and writing that are most popular with many boys, stories that include violence, parody, and bodily humor.

The decision (if it is a conscious decision) to exclude these forms of reading and writing is based on a number of deeply held beliefs: that there is a contemporary crisis of declining moral values and academic standards; that the influence of popular culture is a cause as well as a symptom of this decline; and that the intrusion of this culture into the classroom would be wasteful and maybe even dangerous. Of course, any claim of "decline" inevitably involves a comparison between the current cultural climate and the nostalgic memories of the adults making the complaint. But this narrative of decline was around when my generation was in school, when alarmists worried about juvenile delinquency and the corrupting effects of comic books, *Catcher in the Rye*, and, of course, Elvis.

The elephant in the room, the issue that cannot be ignored, is a deep cultural anxiety about the socialization of boys (a concern that goes back at least to Plato). More particularly, this concern is about boys' perceived propensity to violence and aggression, triggered by suggestions in music lyrics, violent video games, and action movies. We sift through the lives of the Columbine killers and come up with rock star Marilyn Manson as an obvious cause for what happened. (For all the handwringing, it's more comfortable to see this threat as "out there" in Hollywood than within the dynamics of households or tied to economic disadvantage that promotes alienation.) The job of schools, then, is to stand *against* these antisocial narratives, to make a stand for more uplifting and humane relationships, to elevate the taste of students to more morally appropriate literature preferences. As appealing, even commonsensical, as this argument appears to be, it is one I want to argue against.

First, there is no clear or logical line connecting reading and writing about violence with acting violently in the "real world." In fact, the great literature promoted by the staunchest educational conservatives, such as the classic fairy tales, is filled with aggression and cruelty, to the point where the originals are often softened for young readers today. It is, in other words, not logical or fair to allow horrific events, such as the Columbine shootings, to lead us to pathologize and police a whole generation of boys and their literacy education. It is also profoundly demeaning, not to mention inaccurate, to depict young boys as simply reactive organisms, triggered to imitative action by media suggestions. This reductive reading of boys is at the heart of my critique. For as we will see, boys almost never simply reproduce in their writing what they have seen in movies or on TV—they transform it, recombine story lines from various media, and regularly place themselves and their friends as the heroes.

This representation of boys as passive dupes of the media quite simply underestimates their capacity to resist, to mock, to discern the unreality of what they see. Watch any group of twelve-year-old boys watching television—watch the ruthless surfing that gives shows literally seconds to prove themselves. Listen to the caustic commentary. I usually leave the room, almost nauseated, as I get segments of a half-dozen shows. For a sneaking second I feel some pity for the writers and producers who have to face this audience, knowing that their shows, if watched at all, will be dismembered.

The core data for the book is a set of student stories and a series of interviews with about one hundred students, boys and girls, in five New Hampshire elementary schools where they had considerable latitude in choosing topics and genres. In these conversations, I tried to explore the sources of their stories, their criteria for good writing, and their views on using violence in their writing. I will also draw on other published studies to ground and extend my own observations. But as in all qualitative research, the true test of what I say will be made by readers who test my claims against their own observations, in this case of young male writers.

I will be making my case unconventionally, juxtaposing Plato and Batman, Rousseau and Britney Spears, *Beowulf* and *Jackass*. The references to classical educational thinkers are essential to the argument I am making because it is too common to ignore continuities with the past, to think of educational problems in terms of crises and precipitous declines—to overrate the uniqueness of our own times. I will argue that there is something egocentric, lacking historical perspective, something inaccurately nostalgic in imagining boys today as so qualitatively different from the boys of my generation or of earlier eras. While media may change, the narrative content of the media is often strikingly consistent. Boys, without knowing it, endlessly replay the hero and monster epics of Anglo Saxons—as do many of their video games. American convictions about progress, decline, change, and impermanence are deeply rooted, but I will try to make the case for some basic stabilities in boys' narrative preferences.

I will also take a more generous view toward the visual media—TV, movies, computer games—that children appropriate in their writing. These visual narratives are often depicted as The Enemy. They are the narcotic that keeps children, particularly boys, from more wholesome and self-improving activities like reading. According to this view, we need to take a stand for a print culture, for serious literature that seems increasingly slow-paced to a generation raised on channel-surfing. In this book I will be joining educators like Anne Haas Dyson to ask if these visual narratives might be viewed as *resources*, as sources for plots and characters, as cultural material that can be put to good use. If TV is the primary entertainment for economically disadvantaged children, as surveys indicate, don't we have an ethical obligation to know and work with—as well as extend—those narrative affiliations? Can we really afford to be TV snobs?

While the primary subject of this book is boys' literacy, the issue of "popular culture"—and its appropriateness in schools— also affects valuations of girls' literacy. Girls will write about sports, and while they claim that boys are more "violent" writers, they are also attracted to horror fiction, in which violence, or its possibility, is an indispensable element. They are also a receptive audience to boys' action stories if they are done in an interesting way—which, as I will argue, is the skillful mixing of humor and action. So the lines are not clear-cut, and I will quote extensively from my interviews with girls and hope that the argument in this book will work to their advantage as well.

Still, the materials that boys try to import must often violate stated or unstated rules of appropriateness. For example, one fourth grader explained his anxiety about using variations of *The Simpsons* plots:

**DON:** There's a lot of stuff in it that I can't do at school. Like a lot of drinking and stuff—but sometimes I get some stuff in. Like the episode tonight was this principal and he was tying his shoe. Lisa, Bart's sister, gives Bart her project. It's the biggest tomato. So Principal Skinner, he's tying his shoe and Bart has the tomato in his hand and he is looking down and he throws the tomato and Lisa goes, "No!" And then Principal Skinner goes, "Ahhh!" "Splatt!"

**TN:** It hits him on the butt?

**DON:** Yeah, it was really funny—I like that kind of stuff.

Don is clearly testing the limits of what he can "bring in": how can he employ *Simpsons* plotlines without appearing too disrespectful to adult authority figures? Has he read it right? Is drinking unacceptable but practical jokes allowable? These boundary lines will be a major subject of this book.

When I was the age of the students I interviewed, we didn't have the options boys today have, whole channels devoted to music videos and subversive humor. But we did have *Mad Magazine*. Almost any male who grew up in the 1950s and 1960s has fond memories of *Mad*; it was, for many of us, an introduction to parody, to irreverence. Unlike the stories we read in school, it seemed written just for *us*, and we enjoyed the subversiveness of passing it around during class, hiding it behind our schoolbooks as we read "Spy vs. Spy" or "Superduperman." The one standard fixture was Alfred E. Neuman, freckled, gap-toothed, and clueless, whose motto was "What, me worry?"

I suspect that some might consider that a motto for this book, since I am arguing for the viability and utility of forms of popular culture that many in education dismiss as inappropriate or worse. I am also crediting kids with the ability to interpret this culture—they are more than the passive dupes they are often made out to be.

But I do, of course, worry.

I worry about bullies. I worry about the narrow construction of masculinity in our culture that views deviance as "queer." I worry about hierarchies that always put athletes on top. I worry about boys who don't fit this narrow definition, who are oppressed by "the boy code." I worry about schools so big that kids get lost in them. And like any parent I worry about the horrific violence that occurred in Columbine and other schools.

But my main worry is about boys who are alienated from school itself, who find the reading and writing in schools unrelated to anything that matters to them. Such boys—and I was one of them—partition their lives into "schoolwork" and "things that really matter." For some, parental pressure and expectations are enough to keep them at it; others simply disengage. I worry about them. And there are a lot of them out there.

But I think there are opportunities for bringing these boys into Frank Smith's "literacy club." It will require us all, though, to ask the central question of this book—what counts as literacy? How can we learn about, appreciate, and make use of the narrative affiliations of potentially alienated boys? How can we tap the interests that exist on the other side of the partition?

I am convinced that these boys can be reached if we are willing to interrogate our own values and open ourselves to a more comprehensive view of narrative choice. If that makes me an optimist—well, I've been called worse.

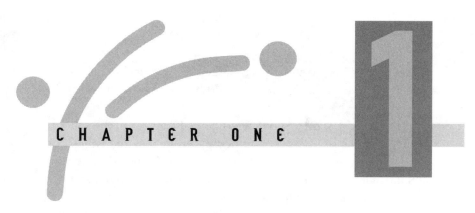

# CHAPTER ONE

# The "Crisis" in Boyhood

Probably the most dangerous mammal on the planet is the adolescent male.

—Charles McCaffery, forensic pyschiatrist, quoted in Kittredge (2001, 8)

In late 2000, a sixteen-year-old Canadian boy was held in juvenile detention for over a month. His crime? Writing a fiction story in the Stephen King tradition about a tormented and bullied student who plants explosives in his school. One section read

> The next day he came to school he was super happy, bouncing along in a hyper/jovial mood, he laughed at the stupid jokes, pretending not knowing that they were intended as insults. He was buddy-buddy with the teachers. Oh just the best of mood. I guess no one knew he had woken up at 5 in the morning and had jimmied the lock to one of the back doors. In addition, he carried 13 packages of C-4 [explosives] and a detonator.

He concludes his story with this sentence: "He decided to detonate at 12:12 exactly. Everyone would be having lunch and having fun."

The student, it turned out, was a recent transfer to the school, where, because of his speech impediment, he was the subject of persistent taunting. Although there was no evidence that he was actually planning an attack, and although he denied to school officials that he had any intention of blowing up the school, he was detained under four counts of a Canadian law prohibiting the uttering of threats. His mother staunchly defended his right to write such a story, particularly in light of the school's inability to stop the bullying: "Of course I wish my son wrote about butterflies or flowers instead of blowing up the school. . . . But he should have the freedom to choose his own style of writing . . . No one ever put Stephen King in jail for writing bizarre stories."

In an action normally directed at repression in totalitarian countries, the authors organization PEN-Canada came out in support of the boy, pledging to raise money for legal expenses. Stephen King himself issued a statement in the boy's defense, concluding that "it has been a time-honored custom to put people in jail or bully them because of their imagination" (Nickerson 2001a, A5).

Although stories like this one have always been troubling to teachers, it is only in the wake of the Columbine shootings that some types of writing and drawing have been criminalized. In a recent Massachusetts case, a twelve-year-old boy was criminally convicted for drawing a graphic picture of himself murdering a teacher. At Boston Latin School, a student was suspended (later reversed) for writing a story that included the killing of a fictitious teacher. Situations that would years ago have been ignored or dealt with privately are now finding their way into our court system. Even writing that is fiction can be read as a convictable offense.

This writing can be troubling, no doubt about it. Fiction can be used as a way to disguise threats and to play out personal aggression. The recent school killings show that even relatively young children, with their ready access to guns, are capable of hor-

rific violence. Teachers are placed in the difficult position of trying to sort out the real threats from normal bluster and playacting.
Even the vast majority of the writing, which does not represent a
personal threat, can create troublesome issues of limits and appropriateness—particularly the writing of boys. Should killing be
allowed in their stories? If the answer is yes, can't schools be seen
as condoning the violent resolution of conflicts? If the answer is
no, how can we deny them the opportunity to mimic the forms of
narrative that they often respond most readily to? How do we balance social appropriateness and boys' attractions to fantasies of
conflict and violence? And who is to decide what is appropriate?
On what criteria? These questions are even more problematical
for female teachers, who themselves may not have experienced
these attractions growing up.

This concern about popular culture and the socialization of
boys is not new. It is a major theme in Plato's *Republic*, particularly
in the section where he discusses the banishment of the poets and
their all-too-human depictions of the gods. Plato saw boys as particularly susceptible to models like Achilles, who could be filled
with self-pity, jealousy, and a thirst for revenge. Plato writes:

> If our young men listen to passages like these seriously and don't
> laugh at them as unworthy, they are hardly likely to think this sort
> of conduct unworthy of them as men, or resist the temptation to
> similar words and actions. They will feel no shame and show no
> endurance, but break into complaints and laments at the slightest
> provocation. (1955, 143)

Plato anticipated the issues in the current debate. He saw educators as working in an environment where the popular culture, at
that time the well-known stories in the *Iliad*, was undermining the
moral efforts of education. This is the case because boys are so susceptible to these models; they cannot "resist the temptation" to act
as the heroes act. They cannot mediate between a literary model
and personal conduct. Education, then, must stand in opposition
to popular culture, even to the point of censorship.

It was the same concern that a much less philosophical Aunt Polly has in *The Adventures of Tom Sawyer* when, unable to locate Tom, she exclaims, "What's gone with that boy, I wonder?" The answer is that Tom is immersed in the sensationalist popular culture of his day—dime novels. He had read, or was at least very familiar with, Ned Buntline's *The Black Avenger of the Spanish Main*, and spent much of his time with his friends teaching them the rules of piracy:

> Oh, they have a bully time—take ships and burn them, and get the money and bury it in awful places in their island where there's ghosts and things to watch it—and kill everybody in the ships— make 'em walk the plank.

But then he explains that they don't kill the women, who are "noble" and "always beautiful."

In the 1950s the terms of the debate were almost identical, though now the target became comic books, which according the crusading psychologist Fredric Wertham were a major contributor to juvenile delinquency and copycat crimes. The anti-comic furor led to a (comic) book burning in Nebraska, congressional hearings in Washington, and, ultimately, a comic book code that prohibited references to sex and drugs, and any depictions of excessive violence and challenges to authority. Using an argument that would later be applied to television, the violence of comic books was portrayed as the beginning of a slippery slope that would lead to an addictive need for more violence:

> These [comic] books depend on the administration of violent shocks to the nervous system, and just as the drug addict must progressively increase the size of the dose to obtain the same effect, so the sensibilities can become dulled by the repetition of a particularly brutal kind of act, the degree of violence must of necessity increase. (Mauger 1952, quoted in Sabin 1996, 68)

The male readers of comic books were seen as virtually helpless, entirely susceptible to the suggestive violence portrayals; as

FIGURE 1–1  *Post-Columbine Representation of Boys*

completely unable to untangle fantasy and reality. And in retro-spect, some of the reasoning seems downright absurd—like Wertham's claim that the Batman-Robin relationship promoted homosexuality.

The most recent wave of concern about the effects of popular culture on male behavior occurred in the wake of the Columbine killings. The images were indelible—the aerial shots of terrified students racing from the exits, the smiling yearbook photos of the victims—and the young killers. Equally horrifying were the accounts of the casual choice of victims, the slow death of one teacher, who was comforted by students who held family photos for him to look at as he bled to death. These images, these stories were more powerful than any statistical analysis of youth violence (which was, in fact, at a twenty-year low [Meckler 1999]). And in the rush to assign blame, the music, TV, and movie industries came in for much criticism. In the 2000 election, Democratic can-didates focused their attacks on Hollywood (when they weren't collecting contributions from their backers there).

In response, cartoonists depicted boys sitting before their televisions and video screens with wires running to their heads, programmed for violence (see Figure 1–1). Now, suddenly, boys *in general* were seen as prone to violence; they were, in the words of one psychiatrist, the "most dangerous mammals upon the planet." Schools routinely prohibited "any violence" in school writing. One third-grade teacher, when asked what she would do if a child chose to write on a violent topic, responded this way:

> I would probably talk to the guidance counselor. I would also con-
> tact the parents to see where it was coming from. "Is this from TV,
> older siblings, or different things like that?" I don't think I would
> say, "You can't write about it," but I would say, "I prefer you to use
> this type of writing at home." (Schneider 2001, 421)

Not only is this writing banned from the school, it becomes a potential index of psychological dysfunction, requiring the assistance of a counselor. What may at one time have been treated as boyish play is now pathologized.

Two Canadian researchers found these prohibitions firmly in place in schools they examined. They interviewed one fifth-grade boy, an avid hunter—a passion he shared with his father—who could not write about his experiences because they constituted violence.

**D:** Like sometimes when she [the teacher], say she writes, "What did you do on the weekend?" I wanna write like I was shooting gophers or something like that. We're not allowed to write about anything with violence. . . .

**INTERVIEWER:** So when you're asked to write about things in school, do you sometimes find it hard to write about what the teacher asks you to write about?

**D:** Yeah, she just wants us to write about sunny days and stuff like that. (Kendrick and McKay 2001, 12)

I suspect that there is a social class bias in this prohibition as well.

But it is unlikely that any probitions can truly keep "violent" play out of the classroom. In one first-grade classroom my associate, Louise Wrobleski, noticed two boys sitting opposite each other at a writing table, each with a booklet of paper stapled together. Anthony had drawn an army helicopter and a horizontal line for the ground. He jumps up facing Justin and says, "They are shooting the bad guys and blowing them up."

Justin leans over, his eyes flashing, "My guys are shooting the bad guys too. They have bombs." Louise asks if he is going to add that to the story and Anthony says no and resumes "writing." Using the black magic marker he draws an airplane in the sky, a cloud, and a line for the ground. Then he jumps up and springs into action, "Bombs are blowing up the buildings! They got the bad guys! Yeah!" Justin takes his turn, adding action-packed ideas that are neither drawn nor written about. This writing game continues for the twenty-minute writing period.

At first Louise wonders if they simply don't want to expand their writing, until Anthony explains that they can't have violence or guns in their writing. They ask if they can take the writing home to complete the story, but that too is not allowed. And the boys, who actually like rules, choose to follow them.

## Two Stories

My intent in this book is not to minimize the horror of school shootings—nor to simply *defend* all of the forms of youth culture that have come in for criticism. But the crisis mentality that Columbine has spawned has radically oversimplified a complex issue—the role of popular culture as a powerful alternative literacy that attracts boys. By treating this literacy as a drug (or an electrical impulse), this hysteria precludes educators from examining the appeal and meaning these disapproved-of forms hold for their viewers and listeners. It precludes questions about how these primary narrative attractions might serve a useful purpose in schools; in fact, this blanket disapproval encourages a bunker mentality where the visual media is seen as the enemy.

Yet as a country we are attracted to this crisis mentality because, paradoxically, for all its seeming pessimism, it is self-flattering. As a director of a large university writing program, I am often asked to compare today's students with those of earlier decades, and those who ask are vaguely disappointed when I say, sometimes citing relevant research, that I see little difference. They want to hear about a dramatic decline, a crisis. To live in a crisis is to live in a special time, a critical moment in history, one that gratifies a desire to see ourselves as unique. We are called upon to act decisively at a key historical juncture. The end of the Cold War deprived many conservative politicians of the sense of crisis, and one can almost sense nostalgia on their part (many have taken to criticizing teachers—or "failing schools"—as the new enemy within). But the problem with a crisis mentality is that, in addition to reducing complex problems to a single cause, it overstates the uniqueness of the present moment. It blurs important continuities—which leads me to two stories.

In a conversation with my mother, a retired high school teacher now in her late eighties, I mentioned my interest in boys' attraction to violence. She paused, then said rather sheepishly, "I suppose you're going to tell the story about the Easter basket."

"What story? I don't remember any story."

She paused again, not sure whether to go ahead. "Well, remember how you were allergic, so we couldn't give you chocolate bunnies and that kind of thing. Well, we wanted to put something special in the basket, so we gave you a toy gun."

"Mom, you put a toy gun in my *Easter basket*?"

"Yes, we didn't want you to go without."

We couldn't pinpoint the exact year, but I must have received my Easter gun around 1955, the Eisenhower years, a time of extraordinary domestic tranquility. Yet toy guns were everywhere—small cap pistols, bigger .45 replicas with holsters, plastic army rifles. We still have some embarrassing pictures of my cousin and me in cowboy hats and chaps, each of us with a holstered gun; my poor younger brother, who never could choose sides, was an Indian with a cheap beaded headband that held one sick-looking feather.

And on television guns were everywhere, the ultimate arbiter in the lawless West. The most popular evening television show was *Gunsmoke*, followed by *Bonanza* in the early 1960s. In that era of limited choices, one in four teenagers regularly watched *Bonanza*, more than double the audience of the most popular current show for adolescents (as I write it is *Malcolm in the Middle*) (Salamon 2001). We could also see *Maverick, Wyatt Earp, Sugerfoot, The Rifleman, Have Gun Will Travel*, and *Palladin*. On Saturday morning there would be *The Cisco Kid, Hopalong Cassidy, The Lone Ranger, The Gene Autry Show*, and *The Roy Rogers Show*. I watched them *all*. Some of the shows used guns more than others (Roy Rogers and Gene Autry sang too much for my taste), but guns were always there. What I don't remember are *real* guns being around. When I did have a chance to shoot a real gun, at YMCA camp when I was thirteen, I was terrified, shot one round, and have never held a gun since. The line between fantasy and reality was as clear as life and death.

My second story is more recent. My wife and I were touring Ireland and decided to spend some time in Connemara, a mountainous area on the western coast, north of Galway. Connemara is often described as the spiritual heart of Ireland, where Gaelic is still spoken in homes and schools. Traveling on a farm road that skirted the Maumturk Range, I swung a little too wide on a curve in the road so that my tires began to sink into the boggy earth at the road's edge. The car came to a stop, tilted to the left, and no amount of spinning of the wheels could get us out. The car was stuck, the left wheels in over a foot of wet, soft earth—we were literally bogged down.

It was the most isolated spot we had seen in Ireland, like some place in rural Wyoming. According to our map we were in a farm community called Derryvealawauma. Farms stretched to the scenic mountains, sheep dotted the hills. There were farmhouses in the distance, and down the road a young farmhand herded about a dozen cows toward our immobilized car. As he spoke with us, we were joined by two young boys aged about thirteen, the more talkative one named Patrick. The conversation would shift from Gaelic, which sounded like Swedish, to English and back. And I remembered thinking that we had stumbled on something original, the untouched part of this Ireland.

As the farmhand fetched his bicycle to locate someone with a tractor, I began to ask Patrick how he spent his time.

"Sheep. My uncle has a lot of sheep, a whole lot of sheep."

"Anything else?"

"Playstation."

"You have Playstation at your house?"

"Oh, yes, they have American football on it. It's deadly."

"Yeah, it can be a bit slow."

"No, it's deadly good. And basketball—do you know Kobe Bryant? He's deadly."

As it turned out he also rented several movies a week and had recently seen *Mission Impossible II* at the theatre in a Clifden. While lacking the choice of cable channels that his counterparts in the United States would have, he was keenly in tune with American popular culture. For better or worse, Britney Spears belongs to everyone. The farm owner came with his tractor, pulled us out, warned us that the rental car people would look for bog dirt on our car so we should be sure to wash it off, and we were on our way, feeling a little less like explorers in Ireland's primitive west.

What stands out in this incident is my desire to "construct" Patrick as a "natural" boy, uncontaminated by popular culture, in touch with the land, unspoiled. He could be someone who could carry on the traditions of sheepherding and turf cutting. He could be a human "preserve" who could remind us of what we were losing. Patrick, I suspect, wanted nothing of it—he wanted to be part of a global youth culture.

The fact is that many countries with dramatically lower crime rates are wired into the same programs, movies, and music that American children spend time on. Japanese television is exceptionally violent, and shows including *The Mighty Morphin Power Rangers* came from Japan. British television and newspapers are more sexually explicit. To blame youth crime on popular culture is to find an easy target; to quote Claude Rains in *Casablanca*, it's to "round up the usual suspects." This is not, once again, to condone everything children watch or listen to, or to defend the *amounts* of time spent watching TV, particularly watching it alone. Yet these figures seem more symptoms of a larger problem, primarily the nonavailability of parents (because of work, divorce, separation, single parenting, etc.). Between 1970 and 1998 the number of non-marital births increased by 223 percent, the number of single mothers who had not married increased by 364 percent, and the number of children living with unmarried couples increased 665 percent (figures cited in Hacker 2000, 16). It is beyond the scope of this book (and my competence) to analyze these disturbing numbers. But TV watching is more likely the *effect* of these trends (which leave children on their own a great deal) than the *cause* of them. To blame Hollywood and MTV for the social dysfunction in our culture is to practice avoidance.

It is also important to take the long view, the historical view, when it comes to popular forms of "story" broadly defined—rap, MTV video, the Comedy Channel, slasher movies, bodily humor, etc. Seven-year-old boys did not invent fart jokes, although they often act as though they did (for a long time I thought it was an anatomical activity that only boys could perform). Games (like Dungeons and Dragons) and cartoons draw on mythological themes, quest narratives, and medieval settings common in earlier literature. While we might make a clear distinction between high culture (Shakespeare) and low (bodily humor), Shakespeare him-self loved bodily humor, as did Aristophanes, Chaucer, Rabelais, and James Joyce.

It is, in fact, misleading and inaccurate to picture great works of literature as existing *in opposition* to popular and sensationalist writing. As literary critic David Reynolds (1988) has shown, the great writers of the American Renaissance—Poe, Melville, Hawthorne in particular—were keen readers of this material and made good use of it. In the first half of the nineteenth century, the popular press fed an almost insatiable desire for the macabre and scandalous—violent murders and unrepentant criminals, licentious clergy, cannibalism, live burial, witches, and sea mon-sters (sound familiar?). This sensationalism provided material and established a readership for Poe to create his own horror stories and for Melville to write about his great, destructive whale. These writers were not aloof from popular culture—they were deeply responsive to it.

If high culture "needs" popular culture, the reverse is equally true. "Great Literature" is a source of plots, characters, and generally recognized reference points—and it can be an object of satire and parody. The popular movie *Clueless*, later a TV show, rests on a plot derived from Jane Austen's *Emma*, all the while mocking the kind of schooling that would *require* the reading of a book like *Emma*. Cher would surely talk her way out of that assignment, yet in one delicious scene she corrects the snobbish girlfriend of her stepbrother, who misattributes a line from Shakespeare—Cher knows the line because she saw Mel Gibson in *Hamlet*. The great Monty Python series makes a grand mess of the Arthurian legends it parodies. The Marx Brothers needed *Il Trovatore;* the Little Rascals needed *Uncle Tom's Cabin*. High culture is never far away.

Taking this more complex view, we may be less likely to try to dismiss (or ignore) these various forms of (sub)literature. In this book I hope to make a more generous reading of these narratives, not to argue that anything goes, particularly in a classroom, but to move beyond the predominant censorious attitude toward popular culture and open up to the transgressive pleasures of boyhood.

## Ways of Misreading

I use "misreading" to refer to the lack of ethnographic interest in boys' narrative affiliations. By this I don't mean that teachers, in addition to all they do, should become ethnographers or conduct formal research. Rather, I am endorsing a decentered stance that inquiring teachers naturally take, particularly when they confront unexpected forms of behavior or unusual student preferences or learning styles. It is the ability to think beyond the "logic" of normal school performance in order to inhabit the "logic" of the student. One thinks of the young Jean Piaget, working with Alfred Binet on the early intelligence test in Paris in 1900. What interested Piaget was the *rational* processes that led students to come up with

different answers. He thus began his monumental task of defining the logical systems children employ as they develop.

Novelist Alison Lurie compares the study of children to
anthropological study:

> [T]o an adult much of the folklore of childhood may sound trivial
> or even meaningless. This is to make the same mistake that early
> explorers made when they couldn't understand the stories and
> jokes told in other cultures. . . . Anyone who has spent time around
> children and observed them carefully, or really remembers what it
> is to be a child, knows that childhood is a separate culture, with its
> own, largely oral, literature. (1990, 194)

I would add only that increasingly, much of this literature is a
shared visual/musical mass culture. The linguist Basil Bernstein
elegantly points out the centrality of this ethnographic stance for
teaching:

> If the culture of the teacher is to be part of the consciousness of the
> child, then the culture of the child must first be in the conscious-
> ness of the teacher . . . We should start knowing that the social expe-
> rience the child already possesses is valid, and that this social
> experience should be reflected back to him as being valid and sig-
> nificant. (1966, 120)

As a credo for education in a multicultural society, I don't think we
can do better than that.

The trap, perhaps one we cannot fully escape from, is to turn
differences into deficits. It is difficult to step outside our own skin,
outside our sense of the "normal" or "expected" or "good." For
example, when young boys seem to be perseverating on space
stories, it is easy to assume they are getting nothing out of this
repetition—*because we cannot imagine any pleasure coming from it*.
On the other hand, it is easy to feel gratified by students who value
what we value, who like the books we like. In much of the early
writing process work of the early 1980s (e.g., Calkins 1983), it
was striking how "adult-like" the young writers appeared; their

concerns with detail, leads, and what now seem like endless drafting were almost identical to the concerns of the adult writers Donald Murray (1968) described in earlier work. They were writing like us, and perhaps it was the sense of ourselves reflected in their work that we were applauding.

I want to focus on two types of misreading that help create a dismissive and defensive attitude toward boys' popular culture. The first is a *failure to engage*, the unwillingness to imagine the intended audience for a narrative (book, movie, TV show, rock video); it is to be perpetually puzzled (shocked, disapproving) without taking the time to really pay attention. It is to feed on a sense of false nostalgia for the better, purer, more wholesome entertainment of our own youth—which itself was the subject of disapproval from our parents' generation. It is to play out a generational script, to sound tired and old and crabby, to claim to be upholding the standards of our own youth, when we might be trying to imagine our children's turn at transgressive pleasure. What *Mad Magazine* was for us, *The Tom Green Show* is for my son.

We can often see this attitude when cultured adults are sent to review movies that target younger viewers. A movie like *American Pie* earns one star and becomes a cult classic, though its absurd R rating forced many kids to sneak in (which is what my son did—with my help, I may add). For a while my daughter would never go to a movie praised by the *Boston Globe*.

The adult reaction to the second Austin Powers movie, *Austin Powers: The Spy Who Shagged Me*, was another case in point. The nationally syndicated columnist Howard Kleinberg, *while admitting that he had not even seen the movie*, excoriated those who did:

> About the only Oscar that the latest Austin Powers movie ever could attain would be if they are giving one out for bad taste. The insipid film (no, I have not seen it—and will not—but have seen enough of it on TV to know how crude it is) asks a question of moviegoers: Are you obtuse enough to call this entertainment? Did you walk into the theater by accident thinking you were going to see something intelligent in the auditorium next door? (1999)

The accompanying cartoon shows Uncle Sam with his clothes badly frayed; the caption is "The Moral Fiber."

*New Yorker* critic David Denby concluded that the two Austin Powers movies "could only be called crud classics—we call them classics grudgingly, and with a certain loss of self-respect" (1999a, 89). He was especially critical of one Myers character, Fat Bastard, a "grotesquely flatulent Scot—who isn't funny at all. . . ." Perhaps. But a friend once made this comment on male humor: "There's one thing you have to remember. Farts are always funny."

The other form of misreading might be termed a *literal reading* of males' reaction to media. Boys, in particular, are depicted as incapable of mediating or filtering or resisting the messages sent to them by the visual media. The African American scholar Henry Louis Gates noted this problem with the perception of black males who are treated as "dry tinder," ready to burst into flames (i.e., violence) from the smallest suggestive spark. The metaphors of "TV as a drug," as pollution, or, as noted earlier, as an electric shock emphasize the bypassing of any critical (or moral) capacity. To create an analogy: TV is to behavior as electric shock is to muscle contraction. We are talking simple cause and effect here.

Literalism also takes the form of assuming a direct and unambiguous line of causation between the *representation* of aggressive action and the desire to *act* in that way. When violence is banned in boys' writing, the argument, though rarely spelled out, is that the representation of violence (even when fictional) causes more violence. Otherwise why would it be banned? The actual writing *must* arouse a form of aggression (in the writer and audience) that did not exist before the writing, producing an impulse to hurtful action.

I want to explore this literalism by examining the use of male writing in perhaps one of the most influential books ever written on gender differences, Carol Gilligan's *In a Different Voice* (1982). My focus will be on the ways in which she moves from story-completion tasks to generalizations about males and intimacy.

In one of her story tasks, Gilligan asked both male and female students to complete a story from a picture in which two acrobats were working together on a high wire. Although Gilligan fails to provide some of the most basic statistical information for her comparisons (e.g., the number of students being studied and the statistical significance of the differences), she concludes that the men in her study were more likely to emphasize the danger of the situation and to resolve the story with violence, usually with one of the acrobats plummeting to his or her death. By contrast women were more likely (by a margin of 22 percent to 6 percent) to provide nets to ensure the safety of the acrobats.

Gilligan uses these results to support her claim that men and women have sharply different valuations of intimacy. The tendency of the males to cause one of the acrobats to die suggests the danger they saw in the close connection of the acrobats on the wire. They dealt with this danger by "killing" one of them. The women, on the other hand, worked to preserve the intimacy of the acrobats by ensuring that the relationship survived. Gilligan concludes:

> As women imagine the activities through which relationships are woven and connection sustained, the world of intimacy—which appears so mysterious and dangerous to men—comes instead to appear coherent and safe. (43)

By contrast, the men's story-completion pattern signifies a fundamental aversion to intimate relationships:

> From this perspective, the prevalence of violence in male fantasies, denoting a world where danger is everywhere seen, signifies a problem in making connection, causing relationships to erupt and turning separation into dangerous isolation. (43)

If we parse this sentence, the slippage is breathtaking. Beginning with the violent resolution of the story-completion task (which occurred in only two of every five acrobat stories), Gilligan is quickly at the level of "male fantasies" in general, where danger is everywhere. As the sentence continues, she shifts from the fictional/fantasy world to the real-world tendency of males to have difficulty forming and maintaining relationships. In a stunningly literal reading of the male stories, she equates the fates of the acrobats in their stories with the men's daily attitudes toward friends, acquaintances, and relatives.

Gilligan's focus, to be sure, is on the responses of females, to show their logic and to treat their lack of violence as something other than a form of repression. She attempts to explicate the *different* moral developmental frame that women bring to these tasks. But it is difficult to read her interpretations of male responses as anything more than crude reductions that portray men not simply as "different" but as lacking the capacity for the moral affiliation that any cohesive society must depend on. Males are not simply "different"—they are dangerously different.

How else, then, might we read these acrobat stories? The males who highlighted the lack of a net may have been working from their own sense of story, from expectations for what a narrative must do for a reader. In fact, their affiliation was more likely with the reader than with the characters. Working from aesthetic criteria first laid out in Aristotle's *Poetics*, they may have choosen to create tension and resolution, pity and fear. They could use the high-wire situation, the possibility of a fall (or a betrayal leading to a fall), to create a story where something is at stake. I suspect it did not occur to many of them to provide a safety net, not from any real-life lack of empathy, but because the narratives they enjoyed took place in an unsafe fictional space.

One might also argue that the tendency of female participants to avoid conflictual narratives could be read in another, less reassuring light. Deborah Hicks (2002) demonstrates that an "ethic of niceness" can be profoundly limiting for young girls who need to explore alternative gender positions that might allow them to express anger, frustration, and resistance. Girls can be trapped, or at least limited by, a story type in which love, happiness, and material comfort smooth over the tensions of lived experience. Jane Miller (1996) claims that narratives with "bad girls" as leading characters can create space for reimagining gender roles, and Ruth Vinz (1996) has shown that girls' attraction to gothic fiction and vampire stories may represent just such a reimagining. In other words, resolving potential story tensions with safety nets and nonconflictual plots may be an index of moral connectedness, as Gilligan claims, but it might also be a measure of perceived gender restrictions.

But even this speculation, removed from any direct knowledge of the writers and contexts, is suspect. Researchers in literacy have increasingly stressed the necessity of reading student work in the context of its production and reception (e.g., Dyson 1993)—something Gilligan manifestly does not do. The intentions of the writer cannot be read from a text, bracketed from the social networks of collaborators and readers. These researchers argue that we must pay attention to the "text event," and not simply to the text. The study of boys' writing has particularly suffered from this bracketing; their narratives are read as endorsing individualism, aggression, and the violent resolution of disputes. Yet the writing of these "violent" stories may have involved playful collaboration among clusters of friends. Dyson calls this camaraderie the "social work" of literacy.

The situation seems analogous to an informal chess group that my father was part of for over twenty years, an odd group that included the owner of the major clothing store in town, and a German emigré—a veteran of World War I, left for dead on the battlefield—who made most of the false teeth in the county. On occasion they were joined by one of the town's leading plumbing contractors. I suppose the "text" of these meetings would be the games, intensely competitive and obviously based on medieval warfare. They played to win, no doubt about it. If my dad made a bad move, Mort Preis would invariably smile and say, "You're in trouble now, Morrie."

But it is an entire misreading of the situation to generalize that the *relationships* among the players were predominantly aggressive. These weekly meetings sustained the deepest and most loyal friendships my father ever made. The group gradually dwindled to two, my father and Mort, who continued playing even as his body was being consumed by cancer and he had to be helped up our front steps. With his death, the chess club ended.

## The Minefield

In this book I hope to weave my way through the ideological landmines in the field of gender equity. The debate in this country has been driven by two emotionally charged crises. The first was the equity crisis of the mid 1990s, which was given national visibility by the AAUW report *How Schools Shortchange Girls* (1992) and Sadker and Sadker's *Failing at Fairness* (1995). These reports documented a set of schooling practices, intentional and unintentional, that consistently favored male students. Consequently, "equity" came to mean redressing these institutional biases, although there was considerable evidence at the time that by almost any measure of school success, females were outperforming males (an issue addressed in Chapter 2). The second crisis occurred after the Columbine shooting. The young killers were portrayed not as deeply disturbed exceptions to the norm of male behavior, but as only more extreme cases of pervasive male dysfunction. William Pollack, a psychologist at McLean's Hospital, crystallized this anxiety, portraying the "troubled male" in his best-selling *Real Boys: Rescuing Our Sons from the Myths of Boyhood* (1998). The boys he describes are deeply unhappy, bound by a code of boyhood that prohibits expressions of feeling or affection or weakness. While the book contains considerable good advice on talking with boys who are alienated in the school culture, Pollack clearly generalizes from his patient population to boys in general. His findings are strangely at odds with the AAUW reports, which consistently argued that there was a "self-esteem" gap, with boys generally feeling *more* confident than girls.

Despite this discrepancy, both Pollack and the AAUW (along with Sadker and Sadker—and Carol Gilligan) became the targets of a scorched-earth critique from Christine Hoff Sommers that first appeared in the *Atlantic Monthly* and that was then published as *The War Against Boys: How Misguided Feminism Is Harming Our*

*Young Men* (2000). The real crisis, according to Sommers, was not a gender gap that disadvantaged girls, nor was it pervasive unhappiness among boys. It was the faulty research that was used to manipulate a trusting public to believe those myths. The culprits were left-wing feminists (particularly Gilligan) whose research, in Sommers' view, failed to meet even minimal standards of statistical reporting, yet was used as the basis for equity reforms in schools, all the while disguising the fact that by any reasonable measure, girls were outperforming boys.

So the gender debate came to be set up on a Left-Right political continuum, with liberal feminists the advocates for girls and members of the educational Right the advocates for boys. While Sommers effectively exposes the faulty generalizations and selective use of research data that became standard in the equity crisis, she retreats from any serious examination of the situation of boys in our schools. Her solutions are right out of the playbook of the educational right wing—character education, single-sex schools, and a rejection of feminized, permissive forms of progressive education (which, despite evidence to the contrary, are perceived by many conservatives as dominant in schools). In place of a solution or even a serious examination, we get the romanticism of the Right, the comforting myth that the answer lies in a retreat to a prefeminist, pre-progressive past.

This debate is clearly dichotomized in an unhealthy, misleading way and I would like to extract myself from it, acknowledging important insights from competing camps:

- The focus on "gaps" tends to pit boys against girls, to emphasize either/or. Yet surely it is possible to focus on boys' difficulties in school *without* rejecting claims that girls may experience different difficulties or inequities.

- Too much of the recent attention on boys tends to pathologize them, to overemphasize a propensity to violence or their deep unhappiness. Too much attention is spent on "rescuing" boys who have no desire to be rescued. A better solution, con-

sistent with the ethnographic perspective described earlier, is
to focus on forms of narrative (in the broadest sense) pleasure,
to view boys' culture as viable, alive, and worthy of attention.

* In my examination of narrative pleasure I will show the mis-
match between these preferred youth genres—particularly
action-oriented shows and parody—and the accepted and valued forms of school literacy. In fact, as far as boys are concerned, we are clearly in the Age of Parody, where nothing can
escape mockery for long. The Austin Powers movies, after all,
are parodies of the James Bond movies, which were themselves
parodies of Graham Greene and Eric Ambler novels.

* A dismissive attitude can cause adults to fail to appreciate
the inventiveness that goes into much of the successful programming for boys. I suspect more care is taken in crafting the
ranting speeches of professional wrestlers than in writing
some social studies texts.

* This conflict—the relation of popular culture to school culture—is not a new problem. In fact many of the "classics"
(e.g., *Robin Hood*) that traditional educators like William
Bennett want in the curriculum first existed as subliterature.
The key question raised by Anne Dyson is how a school curriculum can be "permeable" to these primary narrative affiliations—as opposed to defining itself in opposition to them.

One definitional question remains. Increasingly, terms like "masculinity," when not pluralized, seem to imply a unified sense of
"maleness" when in fact there are many ways of being a male, and
these are not fixed in biology but subject to change as societies
change. The technical charge laid against this form of generalization is *essentialism*—the claim that differences among groups of
people are due to permanent "essences." Essentialism is at the
root of virtually all forms of stereotyping, and this form of reductive thinking is reducible to this grammatical form:

*(Name of group)* are naturally *(name of trait)*.

Essentialism obscures differences that exist within the named group; it elevates a perceived trait (filtered through the bias of the observer) into a fixed biological endowment; and because this often negative "trait" (e.g., "women are naturally emotional") is seen as permanent, essentialism allows those in power ("men are rational") to rationalize their advantage.

Because women have for centuries been victims of this form of bias, feminists have been sharply critical of some of the gender research that came out in the 1980s (including the work of Carol Gilligan and the widely read study *Women's Ways of Knowing*), which seemed to argue for a gender-based preference for forms of empathetic moral reasoning and "connected" forms of learning. To some, these positions harkened back to traditional social divisions where women's work was to be the carriers of humane culture— the nurturers, the "civilizers" of men. Unfortunately, the charge of "essentialism" is now leveled at almost anyone who makes broad generalizations about gender—even if the person making the generalization is neutral about the causes of the differences.

In the area of literacy achievement, students themselves tend to jump to essentialist explanations of the long-standing superiority of girls—according to the eleventh-grade boys surveyed in one study, girls are just *naturally* better (Cummings 1994). For years the superiority of boys in math was explained by boys' greater "spatial" abilities—an explanation that seems shaky now that girls have almost closed the gap in math. To distance myself from this sort of deterministic thinking I want to present the following explicit caveats:

* Generalizations about gender, because of their scope, are full of holes. Obviously not every child fits them, and most likely no one child fits them all the time. Generalization about gender *at best* can only describe tendencies and patterns—not deterministic limitations.

● While it seems to me naive to rule out *any* place for biological influence in the way boys and girls behave, it is more useful to view gender roles as social constructions, as tacit social invitations to define oneself in a certain way. As such, they are subject to change.

● There is no monolithic "role," no agreed-upon way of way of "being" a boy or girl—and often the various roles are in conflict (see, for example, Hicks 2001).

● While no one is so radically "free" as to be able to create a self outside the influence of these various cultural invitations, there is a measure of freedom (and thus responsibility) involved. The media portrayal of boys as passive slaves of an all-powerful media culture understates their power to accept, reject, and mock parts of the media culture.

But even if masculinity is viewed nonessentially, as a construct, a social invitation to a way of being, it is important to acknowledge how resistant such constructs are to change. That's why these gender roles often seem to have the stability of biological traits. And that's why efforts to remake boys, to create liberal utopias in which competition, violence, and aggression are banished—in which every story has a safety net—will be met with extraordinary resistance.

The social historian Nicholas Lemann has created the most indelible image of the current gender debate. He closes his account of the Sommers-Pollack battle as follows:

> Pollack and Sommers share an ironclad, deeply worried view of boys, and a desire to send adults with the proper views into boyspace to coax them along in the project of becoming their true selves. One imagines behind each of them a great army of onward

marching adult faithful, prepared to enter this latest engagement of the gender wars. And teen-age boys—standing around innocently in their cargo pants with dorky little moussed peaks at the hairline, lumps of Sex Wax in their pockets, headphones blasting Eminem into their ears—have the misfortune of being in the way. (2000, 83)

These are the boys we want to invite into the "literacy club." But the field is crowded, filled with other invitations, and if these boys do choose to come in, they will be bringing in some pretty weird stuff.

# Making Sense of the Gender Gap

"I just want to be average."
—A male student quoted in Mike Rose's *Lives on the Boundary* (1989)

W hen I was in fourth grade I set the record for being sent out in the hall three times in one day, a record that stood until Molly Tucker, incurable giggler, made it four. Our teacher, Elsie Mae Rickenbrood, seemed to us as stiff as her name. Her class work was an endless succession of exercises in handwriting, arithmetic, and answering comprehension questions. I particularly remember the multiplication of three-digit numbers, endless, sickening rows of them. To this day I still get a tight feeling when I see worksheets like the ones I did, and I still remember the time school ended: 3:15. I would silently cheer on the clock in our room, which would abruptly click forward. Then I waited, much too long, for the next click.

One day when I was especially restless (I may have already made a trip to the hallway), I could see Miss Rickenbrood circling to the back of the room. I wasn't aware of having done anything in particular, but I knew her eyes were on me. After a few minutes she leaned over and whispered in my ear, "Tom, would you like to go outside and run?"

I was stunned. To go outside and run? On my own? When it wasn't recess? What could have possessed this woman to ignore all school rules and allow me to run? I said yes and quietly went to put on my coat. As I recall, I didn't actually run in the play-ground (people would be watching from inside the building), but stood outside the doorway, in the cold, marveling at my freedom. I returned to class after about ten minutes, settled for the rest of the day.

I've always wondered why she did it. Was she simply exas-perated? Or, as I now think, did she have a moment of insight into my need for activity—and decide she was willing to risk breaking a school rule to show me that, despite all appearances, she *understood*.

Miss Rickenbrood retired after that year—word had it that our class had something to do with it. A couple of years later when I was selling blackberries, I came to her door. She looked even smaller than I remembered, but just as stiff and erect. I don't think she remembered me, which is maybe just as well. I felt an urge to tell her I was sorry for what our class had done, the trouble I had caused—and to remind her of that afternoon when she let me run. But I just thanked her as she declined to make a purchase.

When the equity crisis of the 1990s became front-page news, I found myself incredulous at claims that schools favor boys because my own experiences had been so diametrically different. The boys I went to school with shared the conviction that the girls had the advantages. The girls seemed (we never understood why) much more able to work within the school rules, Molly Tucker being an exception. The orderliness of their work gained the praise of the teacher. They were the teacher's pets, the ones who would crowd around her on Mondays just to talk about their weekends. And for six long years it was always a "her"; I remember the longing for a male teacher who might join us at recess, who might punt footballs so high in the air that we could test our bravery by trying to catch them. Only later, much later, did it dawn on me that this "good girl" role may have been restricting to the girls as well, but at the time it seemed they just "fit in" better. If schools had been designed to favor boys, they wouldn't have looked like the ones we attended.

Autobiography is a fallible, but probably necessary, beginning point for any study of gender. Our memories contain the galvanizing moments that move us to write, old irritations and frustrations that remain surprisingly active. Yet a set of memories, filtered over forty years, is a partial and shaky foundation indeed. The boys I grew up with were naturally oblivious to the privileges we had because they seemed like "natural" entitlements. At recess, the boys colonized almost the entire playground as well as most of the sports equipment, our claim indisputable (still a common practice, according to Barrie Thorne [1993]). We played touch football while the girls huddled near the school, endlessly jumping rope—or simply just standing around talking to the teacher. This territorial advantage never felt like an advantage, certainly not an unfair one. It was, to us, an inevitable partition of activity.

Even in class we benefited from a double standard when it came to physical activity, to bodily performance and clowning. In her superb study of gender and play, Thorne describes how students use their bodies as expressive instruments to counteract the constraining rules of school:

> I came to relish kids' playful uses of their bodies, their little experiments in motion and sound, such as moving around the classroom with exaggerated hobbling or a swaggering hula, bouncing in a chair as if riding a horse, clucking like hens or crowing like roosters, returning to a desk by jerking, making engine noises, and screeching like the brakes of a car. They wrote on their bodies with pencil and pen and transformed hands into gameboards by writing "push here" across their palms. They held contests to see who could

push their eyeballs farthest back and show the most white, or hold
their eyes crossed for the longest time. . . . These moments struck
me as little cases of imagination in dryly routinized scenes. (15–16)

While Thorne is not describing behavior that is exclusively male,
boys clearly have greater claim to it. All one has to do is watch the
ways boys can disrupt a "simple" single-file walk to the cafeteria.

The activities Thorne describes all sound familiar to me. The
trick was always to bring the "outside" back into the school building, to run in the hall, to jump and try to touch the light fixtures or
door jambs, and to find any excuse to generate a throwing game—
paper airplanes, pencils, erasers, books, spitballs. It was a test of
alertness to suddenly pitch a book to a friend with the split-second
warning "Catch." The mundane routines of schooling were in this
way transformed into tests of physical skill, to the exasperation of
our teachers. But we were also bringing recess in with us. The
challenge was to take our behavior right up to the line of serious
trouble and escape punishment. We disapproved of the kids who
went too far, just as we looked down on those too timid to contest any part of school, those who didn't go *far enough*.

While we boys may have been performing for the girls, we
never expected them to be more than audiences, or perhaps helpless targets when we tossed an eraser toward them and watched
their panicked attempt to catch it. I don't believe it ever occurred
to us that this behavior, tolerated to a point, could be conceived as
a privilege, as a performative role that was denied to the girls. It
didn't occur to us that by calling attention to ourselves we were
taking attention away from them, that we took up more room in
the teacher's field of vision. It didn't occur to us that by bringing
the playground into the classroom we were expanding the territory in which we might claim advantage.

And it never remotely occurred to us that Miss Rickenbrood
may have felt as trapped in that class as we did. She may even have
felt trapped in her profession, one of the very few open to her when
she began working in the late 1930s, one that her unmarried status allowed her to continue in. Spending each day with ten-year-
olds may have been as distasteful to her as it was confining to us.

When she bent down to ask me if I wanted to get out and run, she may have had more insight into confinement than I ever gave her credit for.

I begin with this long recollection to reinforce a point made earlier: The issue of gender privilege is complicated, in part because privilege becomes invisible to the holder of that privilege. Even attempts to raise the issue of boys' difficulties are often received skeptically by many feminists who have worked so hard to expose the bias against girls, like the ones I have described above. Nothing is more troubling about the gender debate than the fact that is has *become* a debate, pitting males against females. Which is *really* the disadvantaged group? As if there can only be one "winner" in this deficit contest. In fact, it is logically possible, not to mention probable, that advantage cuts a number of ways. Given the historical advantage of males in our culture, any claim for male disadvantage must proceed respectfully; it should not dismiss legitimate claims about biases against females, particularly in the area of performative "rights" in the classroom.

In this chapter I will review the various claims about gender gaps, attempting all the while to avoid an either/or orientation. While I will focus on areas of literacy performance, I will look at other issues related to literacy—specifically, gender differences in classroom participation (a central issue in the Equity Crisis of the 1990s) and in changing trends in college admissions at the end of the millennium. This review of factual empirical claims about gender differences will form what I hope is a reasonably sound basis for the exploration of difference (and advantage) in subsequent chapters. This will *not* be a complete review of the huge literature on the topic. Rather, I will selectively attend to the most definitive and influential studies on the topic.

## Inequities in Teacher Attention

For the past few years my wife, a second-grade teacher, has come home with stories about the behavior of particular boys in her classroom. There were periods when they were pissing on the floor of the boys' bathroom, or using rulers as extended penises, or when one gave the finger to the teacher's aide. Or the many times they refused to work, or disrupted group meetings and had to be sent to their seats (and later to the principal's office). I felt intimate with these boys I'd never met, and would greet my wife, when she came home, with, "Well, how were Simon and Adam today?" I both marvelled at and was appalled by the way these boys controlled the classroom climate, and even the conversation at our dining room table.

Each year there is some version of a Simon or Adam, a boy or groups of boys who take an inordinate amount of my wife's time and energy, needy troubled boys who must be under constant surveillance. This attention doesn't even end when they go home, because there are the regular phone calls and referral meetings with parents, who are often frustrated as well. In the meantime I hear much less, often nothing, about the nondisruptive students, the quiet, efficient workers, the good citizens. This discrepancy has been a key feature in the equity debate of the 1990s—the girls can fade into invisibility as the Simons and Adams take over the teacher's radar screen.

Myra and David Sadker brought this inequity to public attention in their influential book *Failing at Fairness* (1995). They detail the various ways in which boys dominate the teacher's attention (e.g., calling out answers without being "called on") while girls wait patiently, often futilely, to be called on. The Sadkers conclude:

> Girls receive less, less help, and fewer challenges. Reinforced for passivity, their independence and self-esteem suffer. As victims of benign neglect, girls are penalized for doing what they should and lose ground when they go through school. In contrast, boys are rewarded for breaking the rules; they are rewarded for grabbing more than their fair share of the teacher's time and attention. (44)

This argument came to be generally accepted and used as the basis for equity workshops across the country. It placed great weight on the construct "teacher attention," which presumably contributes to both self-esteem and school achievement.

In some versions of this argument, even negative attention, for example criticism or rebukes from the teacher, is perceived as *advantageous* for male students. In the study *Gender Gaps: Where Schools Still Fail Our Children* (1998), a follow-up to the American Association of University Women's (AAUW) groundbreaking report *How Schools Shortchange Girls* (1992), the authors make this claim:

> Research since 1992 on classroom climate contends that what teachers describe as girls' strengths in the classroom—good behavior, the desire to please the teacher, and general attention to assigned tasks—actually works against them; at the same time boys' poor behavior works in their favor. Teachers direct their attention to students who make noise and cause trouble; generally, these students are male. In contrast, teachers more typically single out girls as ideal students—neat, responsible, and quiet. (46–47)

The logic of this claim holds only if we assume that "teacher attention," *whether positive or negative,* is an unquestioned educational "advantage" for boys. I find it hard to believe that anyone who has regularly been on the receiving end of criticism and reprimands could make such a claim.

In fact, there is an extensive body of research to show that this "misbehavior" is perniciously disadvantageous for racial minorities, particularly black males, who are quickly typecast as troublemakers and who are regularly consigned to low-achievement groups from which they never escape (Rist 1970). Behavioral traits—politeness, style of dressing, speaking out of turn, loudness of speaking voice—are regularly translated into cognitive assessments and expectations of school success (Hull et al. 1999). In Ann Ferguson's ethnographic study of black fifth and sixth graders designated as "troublemakers," we can see the fundamental and tragic incompatibility between their school identities (shaped by the very attention the AAUW report sees as advantageous) and the school culture. Ferguson trailed and interviewed students who regularly visited the detention room in their middle school. One of them, Reggie, describes a typical encounter in class:

The teacher says [he mimics a high-pitched fussy voice], "You're not the teacher in this class." And then I say [adopts a sprightly cheeky tone], "Oh yes I am." Then she say, "No you're not, and if you got a problem, you can just leave." I say, "Okay" and leave. (2000, 177)

Reggie may have maintained his status as a talented performer, unwilling to back down before the teacher. He may have received "teacher attention," but as Ferguson argues, his defiance only reinforced his exclusion from the classroom culture. Reggie will leave the class, and then what? Wander slowly to the detention room. And after that, when he can finally leave school altogether, with no marketable skills, what are his options? Statistics on the incarceration of African American males would suggest he is heading toward the prison system.

Up to a point, the AAUW argument is reasonable, simple common sense. Teachers who must continually monitor the behavior of a few boys have less attention to give to more cooperative students, male and female. It's one reason many teachers choose to work in private schools, often for less money, because these schools have the power to exclude disruptive students. It is also a sound democratic principle that all students should feel comfortable participating in classroom talk. Reformers like Myra and David Sadker have helped teachers monitor this participation better; they have also encouraged alternatives to the standard classroom "discussions" that rest on handraising, bidding for the teacher's attention, and publicly displaying knowledge—a self-assertive game many students do not like to play (see, for example, Philips 1983).

These reformers, it seems to me, are less successful at showing *what educational advantage boys gain from attention-getting behavior*. If this behavior allows boys to monopolize classroom instruction, one might expect some differential in educational achievement. If, as the Sadkers claim, boys are offered greater educational challenges because of their greater visibility in class, there should be some payoff. Yet the Sadkers note in passing that "On the surface, girls appear to be doing better, they get better grades and receive fewer punishments than boys" (44). In fact, girls receive better grades in *all* subjects—including math (Cole 1997, 18). If these grades are rewarded for mere conformity, this "advantage" might seem an illusionary one. But since grades are a key currency in schools, it is possible that success is this area is more than a "surface" achievement. In a major study of gender difference, the Educational Testing Service (ETS) makes this claim about grades:

> Some people disparage grades as subjective and unreliable and favoring students who are "nice" and "compliant." Given that grades have consistently been found for decades to be one of the best predictors of academic performance after high school, we seriously doubt the appropriateness of the disparagement. (Cole 1997, 19)

In other words, superior grades reflect more than meek compliance; they are indicative of mastery and of the study habits needed for mastery. They measure something important.

Another interpretation of this disparity in "teacher attention" would go as follows: The greater attention to boys may not have much of an educational payoff. To the extent that this attention is negative, it reinforces the counterproductive "troublemaker" or "clown" identity the student has come to assume. In a sense, it "rewards" that identity, which is not the same thing as conferring educational advantage. Even more positive attention (e.g., calling on boys more often than girls) may not be the great advantage it has been made out to be, because success in school (and, one might add, in the workplace) is dependent on other traits—perseverance, goal-setting, enjoyment of reading and writing, ability to collaborate, and attention to detail—none of which are really fostered in discussions where students bid for the teacher's attention. In the next section we will look at various national assessments that focus on the achievements of boys and girls, particularly in the areas of reading and writing.

## Where the Boys Are

In *Failing at Fairness*, the Sadkers paint an alarming picture of girls falling behind their male peers, particularly in the areas of math and science. They point out that girls begin school with an advantage in virtually every academic area, yet around middle school they begin to lose ground:

> Female test scores begin to descend around middle school when the girls are overtaken by the boys. Girls' test scores continue their downward slide throughout the rest of their education. In science, the lead enjoyed by elementary school boys widens in middle school and is further expanded in high school. The longer girls stay in school, the further behind they fall, especially in the critical areas of mathematics and science. (138)

In fact, the reports from the 1996 National Assessment of Educational Progress show an entirely different pattern for achievement in mathematics. While boys held a slight advantage in fourth grade, the researchers found *no statistical difference* between boys and girls in the eighth and twelfth grades (NAEP 1997). The 2000 results show that small differences favoring boys still exist, though both genders have made significant progress. For example, the percentage of eighth-grade girls performing at the "proficient" or "advanced" levels has gone from 14 percent to 25 percent. This improvement is a real tribute to the many teachers and counselors who have helped convince a generation of girls that they should not shy away from work in mathematics. Males, however, outnumber females in the top 10 percent in math and science (and in the bottom 10 percent).

The Educational Testing Service conducted a meta-analysis of fifteen difference assessments (including the NAEP). The results are shown in Figure 2–1. By far the largest gender gap occurs in the area of writing, where by the eighth grade girls perform 0.6

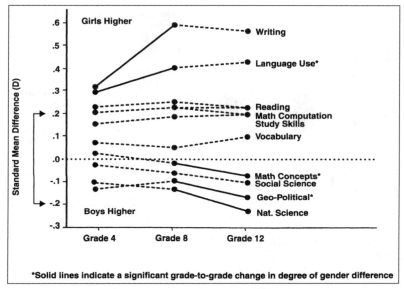

FIGURE 2–1 *Trends by Subject, Fourth Through Twelfth Grades*
*Source:* Educational Testing Service Gender Study

standard deviations better than boys; this gap is *six times* larger than the gap in math concepts, where boys hold a very small edge.

Another way to look at the magnitude of this gap is to compare it to the differences in writing performance of ethnic and racial groups. In the 1996 NAEP assessment for eighth graders, white students outperformed black students by 29 points (on a 500-point scale) and Hispanic students by 21 points; females outperformed males by 25 points (Campbell, Ubelki, and Donohue 1997, 167). In other words, the gap between females and males is comparable to that between whites and racial/ethnic groups that have suffered systematic social and economic discrimination in this country.

In Figure 2–2 the persistence of this difference is clearly displayed. Between 1960 and 1990 the differences in science and mathematics closed dramatically—had the 1996 data been available, the gap shown would be even smaller, perhaps nonexistent in mathematics. Yet the difference in writing remained consis-

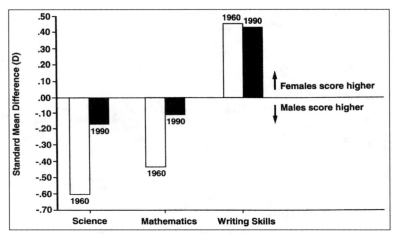

FIGURE 2–2  *Gender Difference in Three Subjects, 1960–1990*
*Source:* Project Talent and ETS Gender Study

tently high. This persistence leads to a few key questions: Why have some of these differences been more amenable to change than others? If we discount the "natural" biological explanation, we need to ask what culturally constructed versions of "masculinity," what educational practices contribute to the stubborn deficit in reading, and particularly in writing. This book will attempt to shed some light on these questions.

## Male Call on Campus

In the equity debate much was made of the unfairness of standardized tests, particularly high-stakes tests like the SAT, which carries so much weight in college admissions. The ETS looked specifically at this charge and concluded that if *only* the SAT were used, there would be a slight underprediction for women. The SAT and tests like it may fail to measure some of the behavioral traits (punctuality, goal-setting, ability to work in groups, etc.) that have contributed to the school success of female students. Their grades in the early college years are slightly better than their test scores would have predicted. But colleges and universities typically use test scores *in combination* with grades (still the single best predictor of college performance). The ETS study found that using both measures leads to remarkably accurate predictions for both genders.

In fact, a remarkable transformation of the college population was well underway as the equity debate raged. In 1970, 43 percent of degrees were awarded to women; by 1997, the percentage had increased to 56 percent, effectively reversing the ratio from 1970. Nationwide, this split is now about 55:45 and is expected to approach 60:40 by the year 2010; it has already reached that proportion at the University of Georgia, the University of Florida, Boston University, and the University of New Hampshire (2002 *U.S News and World Report* rankings). This gender gap is particularly sharp among African American and Hispanic students, where the ratio often approaches 2:1.

I spoke with an admissions officer at my university about this pattern. His job is to visit schools throughout the New England area to recruit and answer student questions. "It's striking," he said. "The young women usually have some good questions, like if it's possible to double-major in business and psychology. You know, specific questions that aren't answered in the catalog. But guys will often ask something like, 'Do you have engineering at your school?' I mean, it's there in everything we send out."

## Reading the Self-Esteem Gap

To this point I have focused on achievement comparisons, and not on *self-perceptions* of achievement, what might be called academic self-esteem. One of the key findings in the influential AAUW study *Shortchanging Girls, Shortchanging America* (1991) was a decline in girls' confidence and self-esteem over the school years. In other words, although girls as a whole outperform boys in all school subjects (including math), they tend to discount that success and develop negative attitudes toward their own capabilities, particularly in the areas of math and science. Comparative studies of gender and self-esteem consistently show a modest but definite advantage in favor of males.

One recent advance in the study of self-esteem attempts to break the global concept of self-esteem into "domains" or categories. In one large study of self-esteem among adolescents, Teri Quatman and Cary Watson (2001) found a pattern of advantage in favor of males, particularly in the areas of family relationships and personal attractiveness. Interestingly, they found no significant difference in the area of academic self-esteem. Females reported better behavior in class; they rated themselves as more conscientious and harder workers than the boys did. They received higher grades than the boys. *Yet the boys claimed to be more satisfied than the girls with how smart they were.* The adolescent girls in the study did not reap the self-satisfaction their achievement would seem to merit, while boys took satisfaction that was not firmly grounded in real achievement. One might read this result as a problem with women's self-esteem—or as a lack of realism in the males' self-assessment.

While I believe that the AAUW points to a real problem that must be addressed—how to help girls be more confident in the capabilities in traditionally "male" subjects—I want to raise two cautions about these claims. First, a comparison of self-esteem is extraordinarily difficult because boys and girls employ different codes, and are subject to different sanctions, when expressing personal inadequacy. It is, for example, well documented that males are less likely to acknowledge personal difficulty, and are much less likely than females to seek help or advice (Jamsen 2001). By contrast, females can often assume a self-deprecating tone that may overstate their level of concern. Donald Murray (1982) noted this gendered pattern in students' self-assessment of writing. So when both are asked to agree or disagree with the statement "I am good at math," two very different dynamics may be at work. The boy may agree with the statement to avoid admitting weakness or inadequacy, and the girl may tend to disagree because the statement appears uncomfortably self-asserting. To read their answers as equivalent is to ignore powerful gendered conventions for acknowledging difficulty. Researchers in self-esteem and gender (e.g., Quatman and Watson 2001) typically claim that the use of anonymity eliminates this possibility, but one wonders how it can be. If self-esteem is so strongly related to gender, why would it be reasonable to assume that males and females will acknowledge self-esteem *in exactly the same way?*

The AAUW report states that "the overall structure of self-esteem is similar for girls and boys" (10, 11), yet within a few paragraphs the authors point up a glaring, almost disqualifying, exception:

> For elementary school girls, in fact, academic self-esteem is the most important aspect of self-esteem; yet it is for them an already negative force. Fewer than half the girls in elementary school (49 percent) say they feel pride in their schoolwork, and that percentage drops 32 points to 17 percent in high school. (The percentage of boys who are proud of their schoolwork also drops between elementary and high school, from 53 percent to 16 percent—but academic pride plays a much smaller role in the structure of boys' self-esteem.) (10)

In other words, this decline matters more for girls *because school matters more to them*. It matters less to boys *because school matters less to them*.

In fact, boys often feel that an open show of enthusiasm for schoolwork, particularly in the language arts, can undermine their identity as a "real boy." When I was teaching English in an inner-city Boston school in the early 1970s, I was struck by the tightrope that the African American boys had to walk, maintaining their identities as tough defiant males and *at the same time* cooperating with a white teacher. I recall vividly the performance Butch Whittaker gave one day. Butch had flunked the first term, and if he flunked the second he would dig himself such a hole that he'd very likely be held back. So he began to buckle down and on one spelling test got an A, his first for the year. After his paper was returned, he stood up and began walking slowly, theatrically, toward the wastebasket in the corner of the room. So slowly that everybody was watching him by the time he got there. Then he tore the paper in halves, then fourths, then eighths, and dropped the pieces into the wastebasket. Once finished, he turned to his classmates and said, "That's what I do with my As." In one elegant gesture, he'd shown us all that grades did—and did not—matter to him. He was both defiant and boastful.

One British survey describes how boys often enjoy the creative side of English, but have to be careful about revealing that pleasure:

> . . . boys also said how hard it was for them to establish networks of readers. They had to be cautious about admitting their pleasure in reading because of negative peer group pressure. . . . What the boys said very forcefully was how hard it was for them to show their enthusiasm openly. Boys and girls asserted that it was easier for girls to be known as hard workers and enthusiastic readers and still retain credibility with their peers. The successful boys felt that they were swimming against the current of opinion among their peers. (*Can Do Better* 1999, 11)

Girls, according to this study, can construct workable identities that include positive attitudes toward schoolwork and literacy. For boys, and particularly African American boys, the role tension is far more extreme. Ann Arnett Ferguson eloquently describes the internal tension felt by a group of students, The Schoolboys, who choose to align themselves with the goals and structure of their school:

> Schoolboys must work to strike a balance between the expectations and demands of adults and peers in and out of school. They experience psychic strain as they weave back and forth across symbolic boundary lines. The ability to "act white," to perform . . . that identity, is a tactic of survival, and a passport to admission to the circle of children who can be schooled. This difference may be rewarded in school by adults but can be a problem in the construction of self

among one's peers and the family and community outside the
school. To perform the act too realistically, to appear to adopt whiteness not as a guise but an identity, is seen as an expression of self-
hatred and race shame. (2000, 212–13)

One way to reduce this tension is to choose sides, to adopt an
identity, or, in the terms of the 1991 AAUW report, a "structure of
self-esteem," in which academic achievement plays little part. In
the long run, that *identity* may be harder to challenge or reconstruct than a decline in self-esteem among girls still *unalienated*
from school.

Several years ago a local fifth-grade teacher decided that as a
year-end award for her class she would buy each of her students a journal. She found some inexpensive but attractive bound
journals with thick unlined pages with fine threads woven in, ideal
presents, she thought, for the summer that lay ahead. Yet when
time came to pass them out she was met with a rude surprise—
the boys didn't want them. They viewed journal writing as so
thoroughly feminized that their standing as males would be
threatened by the possession of such a journal (see Gannett 1992).

The popular media regularly reinforce the impression that
most forms of reading and writing are unmasculine. And I suspect
that commercials with Shaquille O'Neill chasing a page his dog
ripped out of a book are not likely to be convincing. What better
disguise could there be for Superman than to turn him into a
*writer!* One older example of this bias might be the dream
sequence from arguably the best American musical, *Singin' in the
Rain*. Recall that in this sequence, Gene Kelly comes to the big city,
wide-eyed—and *wearing glasses*. In the nightclub he meets Cyd
Charisse, and they perform their famous dance sequence, but only
after she removes his glasses. These glasses mark Kelly as bookish and repressed. With his glasses off, he is cut off from the soli-
tariness of reading; he loses his nerdiness. He gains a sexual
identity and can become her partner. In fact, it's hard to imagine

him performing the scene *with* those glasses. Literacy, boys learn, is not a form of activity, but a pallid substitute for activity; it is not engagement with the world, but a retreat from it. Or as one middle schooler explained to me, "Why should I read about doing things, when I can actually *do them*?" A fair question. We will explore this resistance in the next chapter.

Studies of family literacy show conclusively that reading, particularly book reading, is predominantly a female activity. A recent survey asked students in various grades which parent read most often in their homes. Fifty-six percent reported their mothers read books more often, compared to 5.6 percent who designated their fathers (37 percent said both). By contrast, fathers were perceived to read the newspaper more often by an almost identical margin. So while reading in all forms is not perceived as feminized, the type of reading typically favored in schools clearly is (Pottorff, Phelps-Zientarski, and Skovera 1996).

All forms of print literacy face the challenge of other media, although statistics show it is hardly a contest. The Kaiser Family Foundation study *Kids, Media, and the New Millennium* (Rideout 2000) not only shows the dominance of the visual media, but it shows how boys and girls differ in their allocation of time to these media. Girls aged eight through eighteen spend twenty minutes per day less than boys exposed to the combination of media surveyed (print, CDs, movies, etc.)—a significant figure when *multiplied by every day of the year*. Boys spend more time watching TV (by twenty-two minutes), playing video games (by twenty-nine minutes), and on the computer (by nine minutes). Girls spend more time with CDs and tapes (by twenty-one minutes), listening to the radio (by eleven minutes), and with printed matter (by seven minutes). From these figures we can almost reconstruct the scene: the daughter in her room, headphones on as she does her homework, while her younger brother is at the computer, promising his parents for about the fourth time that he will head up to his room in a few minutes.

To complete the picture, a large recent study of gender differences in the academic help that adolescents receive at home reveals interesting results (Carter and Wojtkiewicz 2000). On four of the seven measures of parent involvement, the researchers found that girls receive more assistance than boys; parents engage in more discussions about schoolwork with their daughters than they do with their sons. They attend more school events for their daughters. And, in general, parents have higher expectations for their daughters (e.g., they were are more likely to expect them to go on to college and achieve advanced degrees). By contrast, parents are more likely to *check* the homework of their sons and to be in contact with their school (the authors speculate that this is for behavioral reasons). Parents also place greater restrictions on the socializing of their daughters. The general picture I draw from this study is of a double standard: The pathway to success for girls is diligent school performance, while boys can still rely on the traditional assurance of male privilege.

What, then, can we conclude about the gender gap in education, particularly literacy education?

Even as the media were proclaiming that schools were shortchanging girls, a sea change was well underway. The traditional gaps in math and science were closing and by the end of the millennium had effectively closed, though boys still outnumbered girls in the top performance ranks. At the same time, the gender gap in reading, and particularly in writing, was wide and unchanging. Boys were far more likely to need remedial reading help, to be discipline problems and receive medication for hyperactivity, to be held back in school. As a group they earned lower grades—even in traditionally *male* subjects (see Smith and Wilhelm 2002, Chapter 2, for a fuller summary of these disparities). As the traditionally all-male professions opened to women (combined with the increased necessity of having two incomes for a middle-class lifestyle), women at the end of the millennium attended college at higher rates than men, and are projected to outnumber them by about 3:2 in 2010. This disparity is greatest among black and Hispanic populations.

Despite this discrepancy in performance, the AAUW reports that women have lower academic self-esteem (though other studies found no difference here). This finding is usually taken as one more example of male privilege in schools—but it can be read another way. Self-esteem is tied to a perception of our capability to meet the standards we and others set for ourselves. The more some form of achievement is tied to critical features of our identity, the more important (and higher) these standards are. The evidence shows that males have higher (or equivalent) academic self-esteem, even though by any measure they do not perform as well as girls. Their high self-esteem may be related to lower self-standards, particularly in what they see as the female practices of reading and writing. This high self-esteem, rather than being a sign of psychological health, may mask their cynicism and lack of commitment to achieving proficiency in school literacy. By contrast, the lower academic self-esteem of girls (even though they admit they work harder and do better than boys) may reflect their higher standards, in some cases their perfectionism. Perfectionism can be a powerful motivating force, yet it rarely allows for the enjoyment, or even the acknowledgement, of real achievement.

This male cynicism about schooling may come from a powerful residual sense of male entitlement—an unarticulated belief that the traits of traditional masculinity (aggressiveness, competitiveness, physical strength, gregariousness, an outgoing personality) will more than compensate for any educational deficiency. These, after all, are the *real* traits valued in the *real* world. Males are more likely to view schooling in general (and specifically literacy) as artificial, even unmanly. By contrast, work, especially physical work, is authentic and valuable. The traits developed on the athletic field and in male friendships are the ones that make the difference. Males can, in effect, make an end run around the educational system and its ladder of credentials. Bart Simpson, despite his poor disruptive school record, will manage to do as well as his high-flying sister Lisa.

This script worked well in an industrial time, when good-paying union jobs were available after high school. Not that long ago a man like Harry Truman could become president with *only* a high school education. And no one can say that male privilege is a thing of the past. But I keep coming back to the opening scene of *The Full Monty*, where those unemployed steelworkers are walking through the deserted factory, their physical labor no longer needed. The rules of the economic game, without their noticing it, have changed.

In the next chapter we will move from a broad statistical analysis of boys' literacy to a closer look at their resistance to school literacy. By quoting resisters—outsiders to the literacy club—I will try to uncover what it is about reading in particular that is so unappealing, so antisocial, so counter to the more embodied acts of learning that occur outside of schools.

# CHAPTER THREE

# The Case Against Literacy
## *A Respectful Meditation on Resistance*

In short, he so buried himself in books that he spent nights
reading from twilight till daybreak and days reading from
dawn till dark; and so from little sleep and much reading his
brain dried up and he lost its wits.

—Miguel de Cervantes, *Don Quixote de la Mancha*

Years ago, when I was a senior in college, I decided to visit
the Widener Library at Harvard during a visit to Boston.
For a small-town midwesterner, this was truly a visit to the holy of
holies, a center of learning that I could barely imagine from the public libraries where I had done "research." True to what I had been
told, access was surprisingly easy, and I climbed the marble steps to
the reconstructed private library of the Wideners, which held, in one
showcase, two central artifacts of Western literacy—a Gutenberg
Bible and a first folio of Shakespeare's plays. I was struck by the
beautiful hand-illuminated letters of the Gutenberg; it was more of
a cross between the old and the new than I had imagined.

Then I went into the main reading room with my thin pack of notecards on, as I recall, Camus and existentialism. The room was darker than I had imagined, with a row of lamps along the center of each table, the only natural light filtering in from narrow windows along the top of the room. A couple of tables away from me was a middle-aged man in a rumpled brown suit and glasses, with not a briefcase but a small *suitcase*, filled with notecards. As I watched he would pull one, consult it, replace it. Spend a bit more time reading. Take more notes on a new card, and then wedge it in to his accumulation. Was this the true life of a scholar, a career I vaguely imagined for myself? I wondered how much time it took to fill a suitcase with notecards, how much time in this dimly lit room, how much isolation, how little human contact? Did he exercise? (Didn't look it.) How did one begin to write from such an accumulation? And ultimately, what kept him at it? It was as if I was watching some ascetic ritual, some form of voluntary holy deprivation, a monasticism that held no appeal for me.

On that morning, I believe I felt something of the mystery of literacy, the incomprehension that the nonreader feels in the presence of the reader. I felt, for the first time, on the *outside* of a practice I couldn't fathom, one that seemed to exact an appalling price. This outsider's perspective is critical if we are to understand the resistance many students feel toward literacy. Too often the argument for reading is made by those who have spent their lives as insiders; the pleasures of solitary reading are so obvious, the value of reading so self-evident, that we fail to appreciate how utterly strange reading is to the outsider.

Most other forms of entertainment and recreation make sense, even if we do not share the skill or even the taste of the person involved. I have no skill in woodworking, but I can imagine the pleasure of a carpenter running his hands over a smooth joint. There is a gratifying interaction between the craftsman and the material being worked; there is the "feedback" of the product as it becomes perfected. Although I have no taste for the music of some rock bands, I have no trouble imagining someone at a concert swept up in the communal pleasure of the rhythms, the music, the lights, the onstage gyrations. I can even see the appeal of Britney Spears and the boy bands. I can imagine a transaction going on. If someone is walking past my house with earphones and a Walk-man, bobbing her head to music I can't hear, the scene makes sense to me. But imagine seeing that same scene never having heard the music—or any music. This is the situation of the liter-acy outsider, particularly in relation to silent reading, an activity that is much more hidden than writing.

In this chapter I will focus on the logic of student resistance to literacy learning, and particularly to the extended forms of novel reading that typically distinguishes the "good reader." I focus on reading because it seems the most hidden of literacy practices. The writer, after all, produces visible text; he or she is the maker of an evolving product, a piece of writing. Except in the most closely defined situations, it is an activity that the writer controls, at least to some degree; it is for many students the most open space they encounter in the school day. By contrast, the reader seems controlled by a fixed order of words, and the "prod-uct" of reading is what? A feeling? Knowledge? The payoff is not at all clear to the outsider.

What, after all, does a reader reveal? Virtually nothing. The absorbed reader is a picture of immobility. She is motionless, not even demonstrating the occasional twitchings or tappings that most humans need to maintain attention when they are sitting for long periods of time. Only the turning of pages every couple of minutes. The reader's face is impassive—there are no notice-able signs of response, no real laughter, rarely even a slight smile. What so stills the reading figure? Printed words, thousands of them, maybe forty or fifty lines per page, also immobile. No pic-tures, no color. Endless combinations of twenty-six letters. And in this almost complete absence of visible stimulation, the reader can remain for hours a time, though when she emerges from iso-lation she may wonder why her children don't like reading as much as she does.

This process mystifies nonreaders like Mick, a high school student interviewed in Pam Mueller's book *Lifers* (2001):

Nothing really goes on. Nothing. Well, maybe you're doing something, but it's just not interesting. You are just sitting there and reading words. You are looking at a bunch of letters and paragraphs and
sentences. You just read. It is pretty basic. It's boring. It's different for
those people that actually like to read. They get a kick out of it. Like
some of the nerdy kids. They really get into it. . . . How can someone
sit around and read for hours and read words all day? I couldn't do
that. I am the type of person that has to keep moving around.

Though Mick acknowledges his own difficulties, he doesn't
exactly glorify those who do read. Their ability to isolate themselves for hours is a sign of their nerdiness—their lack of social and
physical interests.

Nothing seems more unnatural to the nonreader than the isolation reading seems to demand. To concentrate for long periods
of time, a reader of longer texts must have relative quiet and unin-
terrupted stretches of time, ideally a "room of one's own" where
the door can be closed. One self-acknowledged "frustrated
reader" notes that she equates "reading" with a form of punish-
ing isolation (Rosenthal 1995):

I got the message early on that "reading" meant being thrown into
a room by myself—banished. Somebody was going to close the
door and say, "Don't bother me. I don't want to talk to you. Here,
read something. Leave me alone." You had to do it by yourself.
Nobody was going to talk to you. Nobody was there. (30)

If we are in the presence of others, we expect them to respect the
private space we have tried to mark around us, something the
young child does not understand when he pulls the newspaper
down. While many of us have come to love this private space,
many others, and not just children, find this isolation difficult,
unnatural, and ungregarious. In their groundbreaking study of
boys' literacy, Michael Smith and Jeff Wilhelm (2002) stress the
centrality of friendship groups in literacy development; boys read
books recommended by friends, and are more likely to attend to

print stories that can be shared. An ungregarious literacy had no appeal for them.

No one has caught the alienating potential of literacy better than British sociologist Richard Hoggart does in his classic study *The Uses of Literacy* (1957). He paints a picture of the working class "scholarship boy," the first in the family to pass the 11+ exam and go on to selective high school. According to Hoggart, the scholarship boy can be successful only by pulling away from the communal interchanges of the family room:

> He has to be more and more alone, if he is to get on. He will have, probably unconsciously, to oppose the ethos of the hearth, the intense gregariousness of the working class family group. (294)

Because only the family room is heated, he will work at the corner of the table:

> On the other side Mother is ironing, the wireless is on, someone is singing a snatch of song or Father says intermittently whatever comes into his head. The boy has to cut himself off mentally, so as to do his homework, as well as he can. (294)

The scholarship boy, to be successful, has to "resist the central domestic quality of working class life" (295). Moreover, this resistance marks him as a loner.

Of course, children today are not tied to the family room, but they find ways to resist the silence and isolation that independent reading seems to demand; they do so by studying with friends (however inefficiently), working in front of the television, or, if these are prohibited, working to music—anything to break the silence. When I ask my own college students why they avoid the elegant new vaulted reading rooms in the library, they say they can't stand the quiet.

My parents date my birth as a reader to the summer I turned thirteen, when I was diagnosed with Osgood Slaughter's disease, a common ailment in the knee joints that today is left to take care of itself. At that time the standard treatment was the prohibition of all sports that involved running and jumping. Since we had the biggest yard in the neighborhood, all of the summer games took place right below my bedroom, where I methodically worked my way through Dickens, having just bought a complete set for fifty cents at an auction. I entered the world of Fagan and Bill Sykes as the voices from the yard drifted up, though the box elder trees, into my private space. As I recall that lonely summer, the feeling of ambivalence comes back. I had gained a world, but at a price.

## Reading and Silence

Even in U.S. schools, "silent reading," with its necessary psychological isolation, has not always been the ultimate measure of the reader. Around the end of the nineteenth century, students reading *McGuffey's Fifth Eclectic Reader* encountered as their first selection a story titled "The Good Reader." Today that title might conjure up the image of a child, in his or her room, snuggled in a bed, immersed in a Harry Potter book. But the good reader of the late nineteenth century was not this isolated figure.

The story is set in the eighteenth century in the court of Frederick the Great, who has just returned from a hunting trip. His eyes are so tired that he can't read a letter from one of his subjects, so he asks one of his pages to read it. This page reads in a continuous monotone, huddling "the words together in utterances as if they were syllables in a long word." Frederick tells him that he sounds "like an auctioneer" and stops him.

The second page enunciates every word, slowly and distinctly. He too is stopped, and accused of "reciting a lesson in elementary sounds" (maybe the victim of the phonics programs of his day). The king then asks Ernestine, a young girl standing by the fountain, to take a try.

> The two pages were about to leave the room. "Remain," said the King. The little girl began to read the petition. It was from a poor widow, whose only son had been drafted to serve in the army,

although his health was delicate and his pursuits had been such as to unfit him for military life. His father had been killed in battle, and the son had a strong desire to be a portrait-painter.

The writer told her story in a simple, concise manner that carried to the heart a belief of its truth; and Ernestine read it with so much feeling, and with an articulation so just, in tones so pure and distinct, that when she had finished, the King, into whose eyes the tears had started, exclaimed, "Oh! now I understand what it is all about; but I might never have known, certainly I never should have felt, its meaning had I trusted to these young gentlemen, whom I now dismiss from my services for one year, advising them to occupy their time in learning to read." (1879, 41–42)

All ends happily. The son, freed by Frederick from military duty, becomes a famous painter. Ernestine's father becomes the king's gardener. Ernestine continues to read to her neighbors for entertainment and instruction. And the poor pages study reading in earnest and rise to distinction, one a lawyer, the other a statesman—due chiefly to "their good elocution."

This passage presents a strikingly gendered view of reading. The male pages fail to read effectively and need remedial help, while the young girl, rurally educated (like my mother's uncle, whose copy I am using), can succeed. For everyone in the story, reading is the key to Horatio Alger–like advancement. And unlike the contemporary image of the reader, the text is not a novel, but a functional piece of persuasion.

But for the purposes of my argument, the most important feature of this portrait is the very public quality of literacy. The reading of texts is an occasion for gathering, not an act necessitating separation and individualized activity. Ernestine succeeds because she regularly reads letters and circulars to her neighbors, who come together to listen to her. The "good reader" is a public reader, a performing reader, and the goodness of her reading is measured not by the private state she can enter as a reader, but by the public response to that reading.

But by the early 1930s, when my mother began to teach in a

one-room school in northwestern Ohio, the shift to "silent reading" was well underway, probably to the relief of many students who had to listen to readers like the king's pages. Early studies in the eye movement of fluent readers showed that their eyes took in material in large "chunks," demonstrating scientifically that silent reading was more efficient than oral reading. Keeping reading oral, researchers argued, unreasonably slowed the pace with no gain to the reader. The shift to silent reading, then, was one aspect of what Callahan (1962) calls the "cult of efficiency," reflective of the power of scientific management in the early part of the twentieth century.

The shift to silent reading created difficulties in assessment: Once reading had moved underground, leaving no visible or audible traces, it was difficult to determine what was happening. One pair of early researchers put it this way:

> The symptoms of success or failure in [oral reading] are open to direct observation. In silent reading, on the other hand, the observable facts are relatively few and extremely hard to interpret. This obscurity of the symptoms of silent reading make it doubly desirable that scientific methods be developed which will direct the attention of teachers to every discoverable indication of the character of the silent reading process. (Judd and Buswell 1922, 2–3)

Not only did it create this problem for the teacher, but it mystified the process for the struggling reader, who could only puzzle at the gratification a "good reader" experiences. The king's pages could see Ernestine's performance; with the onset of silent reading, the process became hidden. High school sophomore Kevin Clarke puts it this way:

> I guess people who read all the time must get something out of it that I haven't experienced. They must take the material and understand it. I don't know whether they force themselves to read or not . . . (Rosenthal 1995, 39)

In other words, he doesn't have a clue.

## The Inferiority of Reading

I guess they [high school friends] all liked to read a lot. I couldn't figure it out. Maybe they read because they weren't as gifted mechanically as I was and couldn't do things with their hands. I've always been good with my hands. Maybe they read because although they couldn't do something else really well, they could be good readers.

—Todd Martin (Rosenthal 1995, 41)

Why should I want to read about doing things, when I can actually *do them*?

—Devin Bencks, Grade 10

When Juliet informs Romeo that he is kissing "by the book," she is not complimenting him on his literacy. She is drawing on an ancient distinction between knowledge that comes through life experience and knowledge that is passed on in a book. In Shakespeare's time it was common to refer to those who gained knowledge of warfare from books as "book knights" (Amyot [1572] 1941, xxxv). Outsiders to reading, like Todd, often assume that a preference for reading comes from shyness or social ineptitude (read "nerdiness"). Or that, as Todd speculates, it may compensate for a lack of skill in more meaningful, or at least practical, forms of manual labor. How, after all, can an activity that is socially isolating, that produces no visible product, and that makes no visible demands on the body claim to be a *superior* form of learning? By what standard does the vicarious activity of reading trump actual social activity? How can "adventures in reading" be anything but pale imitations of *real* adventures, like jumping from a train trestle or running a 400-meter dash?

These kinds of questions are not the simple rationalizations of resistant readers. In one guise or another, progressive educators over the centuries have consistently expressed anxiety over the centrality of literacy in schools, the ways in which intelligence and learnedness are marked by bookish or purely verbal achievement. In this regard, many contemporary progressive educators in the Whole Language or Writing Process movements seem to have parted company from their more skeptical forbearers. We imagine literacy and learning as so entwined as to be almost synonymous, a position encapsulated in James Britton's 1970 foundational book *Language and Learning*. One cannot read the world without reading the word. But it was not always so.

One of the standard concerns of humanist educators had to do with the relationship of words to things, and the way a language-centered education privileges language over action. Rousseau and Wordsworth felt that the learning of words, definitions, and facts created a showy precocity that was not anchored in experience:

> Thinking he is being taught a description of the earth, he learns only to know some maps. He is taught the names of cities, of countries, of rivers which he does not conceive as existing anywhere else but on the paper where he is showed them. (Rousseau, *Emile* ([1762] 1979, 109)

John Dewey also tartly remarked that students in Moline, Illinois, learned the facts about the Mississippi River without suspecting it was the river that ran through their town. He used the term *over-symbolic* to describe the way learning from books replaced actual observation and social experience.

Anticipating the revolutionary work of Jean Piaget, Rousseau believed that the knowledge of terms and names can create the illusion of knowing, disguising the absence of any operational knowledge. For example, if many of us were asked why an apple falls we would say it is because of gravity, as if that were an explanation. But if pressed, we would realize how circular and unproductive our "explanation" is. "Gravity" is just another way of saying that things like apples do fall to earth. We've simply given a *name* to the phenomenon we are trying to explain.

Nothing was more distasteful to Rousseau than an education for children that centered on reading; books, he flamboyantly exclaims, are "the instruments of their greatest misery" (116):

> Reading is the plague of childhood and almost the only occupation we know how to give it. At twelve Emile will hardly know what a book is. But, it will be said, he certainly must at least know how to read. I agree. He must agree to read when reading is useful to him; up to then it is only good for boring him. (116)

Rousseau suggests that children can learn reading not from books, but from short notes and letters that affect their immediate interests. In other words, reading instruction should be embedded in practical social activity and not treated as a subject of instruction.

The great French essayist Michel Montaigne may have been the most widely read man in sixteenth-century France, yet he too was profoundly ambivalent about the role of reading in a sound education. True verbal skill, according to Montaigne, must be grounded on experience, on activity in the physical/social/political world. Using a distinction that Rousseau would later borrow, he asserted that learning comes primarily from encounters with "things," not "words": "Provided that [the pupil] be well furnished with *things*, words will follow only too easily; if they do not come easily, then he can drag them out slowly" ([1595] 1987, 189). Words after all are symbols, rough designations of some experienced "reality"; a cloistered, literacy-centered education deprives the learner of meaningful referents for language itself.

Both Rousseau and Montaigne had an exquisite sense of the role of physical activity in learning. Montaigne, always quoting the ancients, reminds his readers that Plato saw games, races, sports, dancing, and music making as far more central to educational development than learning from books. Rousseau, acutely sensitive to the negative effects of confinement on children, condemned the contemporary practice of wrapping or swaddling babies (who were often then literally hung on a hook for easy management). Anticipating Piaget by 150 years, Rousseau argued that the physical exploration of the hands was central to later intellectual development—the fingers are extensions of the mind. He even hoped that the older Emile will have "eyes in the tips of his fingers" (132).

Emile is always in motion. Rousseau advocates exercise that promotes general robustness and strength, including in his list swimming, running, spinning a top, and throwing stones. Physical activity also provides occasions for observation, estimation, and comparison, the central perceptual activities Rousseau sees as the precursors to subsequent logical (what Piaget would call "formal") operational thinking. In Rousseau's lengthy descriptions of Emile's education, the boy is never sitting down—and rarely inside.

I make this historical digression to suggest that the opposition to an education *centered* on reading is not something new; it has been shared by the most influential writers in the history of progressive education. For these progressives, reading was an embedded and practical social activity. ("What's it good for?" was Rousseau's mantra.) It was rarely viewed as a separate subject, certainly not one centered on the reading of fiction. In fact, in the most thorough description of Dewey's experimental school, there are more index citations for cooking than for reading (although students read extensively, "instrumentally," in their units); and the measure of the reader was never the capacity to read long novels (Mayhew and Edwards 1966).

Deborah Hicks' thoughtful case study of "Jake," a young working-class boy, shows the unattractiveness of school literacy for someone raised to associate learning, and storytelling, with physical activity. At the end of Jake's kindergarten year she interviewed him, and as part of the interview asked him to tell a story, anticipating he would tell it *from his seat* so that she could videotape it. Here is Hicks' account of what happened:

> Asked to tell a "make-believe story," he created an imaginary track, using gesture and movement to narrate the fictional scene. At one point in the enactment, Jake circled around the classroom to show how the track was configured. In his description of the track, Jake

remained close inside the action, taking the listener with him as he demonstrated the track's spatial configuration. (2002, 112)

His NASCAR race story is more enacted than told, full of sound effects, leading to a climactic scene where Jake, as the race car, crashes into a wall, and Jake, as the driver, leaps out of his burning car onto that of Terry Labonte, his favorite driver. Hicks notes that this story resembles Jake's involvement in Sega football and racing video games:

> During the Sega football game, Jake was extremely physically active. His verbalizations ("I tagged him," "I pushed him out") were uttered in the voice of one actually engaged in the game itself. Jake seemed to be on the field with the players, his whole body moving with every hit. (106)

This mode of storytelling as reenactment is at odds with school conventions for storytelling, where there should be some distance between the authorial "self" and the events being narrated— and where Jake's mode of telling might be seen as disruptive of class order.

As Jake progresses in school, he becomes increasingly disengaged from the expectations to read fictional stories independently and do skills activities. This schoolwork did not correspond to literacy as he knew it at home, where reading and writing were "immersed in the ebb and flow of work, play, and family relations" (118). It was in particularly sharp contrast to the practical, action-oriented ways in which men in his life used their literacy. Jake was on the road to the same kinds of resistance documented in Smith and Wilhelm's 2002 study, the title of which was the claim by one student that reading so disconnected from action "didn't fix no Chevys."

## Literacy and Crowd Management

In my early teaching days at Boston Trade High School, I remember clearly one afternoon when our department chair, Francis Xavier Sullivan, was opening a box of newly published English textbooks. A few years before he had been a teacher at the prestigious Boston Latin School, and he speculated daily on the divine punishment that sent him to spend his last teaching days at Boston Trade.

As he was opening the boxes, Tyrone, a loud but basically good-natured kid with what seemed like a permanent hall pass, walked into Sullivan's room and asked to see one of the new books. After turning a few pages he announced, "I've already read this."

"But son" (yes, Francis called the students, most of them African American, "son"), "these have just come out; I don't think you could have read them."

"I'm tellin' you, man. I read this book before."

"Maybe one like it, son, but this one just came out. See, it's the first edition."

"You just don't believe me, man. I *read* this book."

"I know you think that, but there's no way you could have read it before. It hasn't been in the school before."

"I'll show you I read it man." And then Tyrone opened a few pages then showed them to Francis, "You see. Look. Words. Words. I tell you I read this before."

As Francis told the story, the moral was the impossibility of teaching at Boston Trade (most of his stories tended toward that conclusion). But I thought that Tyrone was taking Rousseau's position—that books are interchangeable sources of affliction. Books are engines for the generation of schoolwork—reading, recitation, answering questions in writing, copying, testing. They are part of the apparatus of regulation; whatever the differences in content, the function of the printed words Tyrone saw was undeniably similar. In that sense, Tyrone *had* read the book before.

While schooling and learning are typically conflated in public discussions of education, both Rousseau and Montaigne argued that confining numbers of students with disparate temperaments and interests in classes with a common curriculum was an impossible task. And even they couldn't have imagined today's public school—no school, at any level, in eighteenth-century Europe had as many students as an average urban high school today. In almost any U.S. town the most densely packed working spaces are the schools, which are more crowded than prisons or office buildings, sometimes the equivalent of small towns housed in a few adjacent buildings. These concentrations require means of crowd control, of disciplining bodies. And literate activity is an essential instrument, as I think Tyrone understood.

When I taught at Boston Trade, I was no means a favorite of the principal, but I do remember one ringing compliment he gave me (or rather my class) one afternoon. He was patrolling the halls and poked his head in, then entered the room. "Mr. Newkirk, this is a wonderful class. Wonderful. What class is this?"

"Tenth-grade sheet metal and welding."

"Well, you're to be complimented on your wonderful work." It was one of the few compliments I received from him. The students that day were doing mindless worksheets on the state capitals. Many of us would pull these out when our students seemed too unruly, or when we just needed an easy period. Not something I'm proud of, but they did settle things down. I suspect that the principal had a visual image of an orderly class, students working diligently, perhaps enthusiastically—but always silently. In a school that could, and did, seem to explode on some days, these classes were an oasis for him (and even for us).

Other faculty at the school built their curricula on mindless seat work. In one history class, students copied notes off the board into small brown notebooks, then, on each Friday, they were given open-notebook tests so they could *recopy* the notes back onto the tests. The teacher was the head of that department and a top-rated teacher in the school. I suspect that in the official curriculum we were claiming to teach reading and writing, when, in fact, we were using low-level literacy tasks to control bodies. Martin Nystrand has documented that in low-track classes this pattern is common; written seatwork is used to occupy potentially unruly students (Nystrand 1997). The pencil in contact with the paper on the desk—that link was the fragile thread that allowed us some form of crowd control. And control was the name of the game there.

Of course, one agenda of schooling is disciplining the body—teaching the students to assume the behavioral characteristics of students. To sit like students, raise hands like students, pay attention like students, work steadily and industriously like students. That is what my principal saw that morning: the *behaviors* of students. He saw encouraging signs that my young welders and sheet-metal workers could perform the role. This behavioral agenda begins early, as Robin Leavitt and Martha Bauman Power show in their study of preschool (1997). They describe typical rituals like rewarding students for sitting properly. In the case they describe, the children are to be seated on the floor, legs crossed, hands folded on their laps, not squirming:

> The children were gathered together waiting to be assigned to play areas. The teacher said to the group, "Whoever is sitting nicely with their legs crossed will get to go first." She then began to call out names and sent children out to play one by one.

She comes down to the last two boys, who were always last in these dismissals:

> She then turned to her coworker and asked in a loud voice, "Well, who do you think should go next, since neither is sitting right?" David and Jim quickly got their bodies into position. The teacher responded, "Wow, that was quick. Now, who do I choose first?" Just then Jim, in his eagerness, wiggled his body. The teacher then said, "Well, Jim, since you moved, David can go first." (50)

Studenthood, these boys are taught, requires supreme bodily

control that seems to come easier to the girls, who are then rewarded by female teachers.

So powerful is the liberatory ideology surrounding reading that it seems cynical to name this underlying behavioral agenda. We are so used to reading being represented as entirely benign and personally beneficial that it may be jarring to view it as an instrument of bodily control. Media scholar Neil Postman, along with Phillippe Aries, argues that beginning in the sixteenth century, childhood and adulthood came to be clearly distinguished and book-centered schooling facilitated the transition from the instinctual exuberance of early childhood into the self-discipline of adulthood:

> In a world without books and schools, youthful exuberance was given the widest possible field in which to express itself. But in the world of book learning such exuberance needed to be sharply modified. Quietness, immobility, contemplation, precise regulation of bodily functions, became highly valued. That is why, beginning in the sixteenth century, schoolmasters and parents began to impose a stringent discipline on children. The natural inclinations of the child began to be perceived as not only an impediment to book learning but as an expression of an evil character. (Postman 1982, 46)

Not only does book reading require a form of self-control, it also trains the student in self-control. The "good" reader is not merely the fluent reader; he or she is also one who has mastered the "natural" willfulness of childhood. I suspect that when parents today lament that children avoid reading, they are referring, at least partially, to the loss of self-discipline and attention control that reading requires.

From a pragmatic standpoint, schools have the task of regulating student movement, of maintaining order in highly congested spaces. Books become instruments of immobilization. To use them properly, or at least conventionally, the reader must be both seated and quiet. We might argue that distinctions should be made between textbooks and literature, but I suspect that Tyrone wouldn't buy it. Both are filled with "words, words, words."

## Reclaiming Pleasure

Many self-acknowledged "poor" readers sound like failed dieters. They'd *like* to read books; they envy their friends who do. They get started with a book, but lose interest and put it down because there are so many more-attractive things to do. Like dieters who feel banished to vegetable land or who drink tasteless milkshake-like drinks, who set out with all goodwill to exercise daily, they simply do not get enough pleasure to continue, no matter how desirable the end product might be. On the big cleanup days, just count how many exercise bikes are out at the curb. The sad, or perhaps not so sad, fact about human nature is that we all have difficulty persisting in activity that gives us little pleasure, no matter how "good for us" this activity might be.

Too often, the value of reading is framed in moral terms, with proponents stressing what they see as the profoundly humanizing effect it can have on us. For example, James Carroll (2001) claims that "contemplative reading is the purest act of intelligence, the main way in which our humanity is expressed—and protected." As we will explore in the next chapter, this kind of statement shades easily into a form of elitism, with readers of a particular sort occupying a higher moral (and intellectual) plane. By what standard do we say that reading is a higher contemplative act than intimate conversation with friends is? Why is our humanity better "protected" by reading than by actual social action in which we help others?

My major criticism with this kind of claim is its motivational weakness; it sets up an ideal end product—the truly moral humane reader—without providing a motive other than a virtuous desire to be good. It's the dieter problem all over again. We can set up the ideal of the healthy body with the proper weight, blood pressure, and cholesterol levels, but unless there is some pleasure in the *means* for attaining this ideal, most people fail to persevere. For example, I have been part of an informal noon swimming group for about fifteen years. This regular exercise is undoubtedly good for us, and sometimes people compliment us on the willpower it takes to keep it up. But willpower has nothing to do with it—because we love to swim. We'd do it if there was no health benefit.

In this chapter I have tried to argue that reading, particularly silent reading, is a meditative state, profoundly and pleasurably engaging for the committed reader—yet mystifying and antisocial to the outsider who has never entered what Sven Birkerts has called "the reading state." He defines this state as a "fundamental and identifiably constant condition that we [readers] return to over and over" (1994, 83).

> In this state, when all is clear and right, I feel a connectedness that cannot be duplicated (unless, maybe, when the act of writing is going well). I feel an inside limberness, a sense of being, for once in accord with time—real time, deep time. Duration time, within which events resonate and *mean*. When I am at the finest pitch of reading, I feel as if my whole life—past as well as unknown future—were somehow available to me. Not in terms of any high-definition particulars (reading is not clairvoyance) but as an object of contemplation. (83–84)

Both Carroll and Birkerts celebrate the contemplative possibilities of reading, but for Birkerts the real attraction is not the moral effect of this contemplation, but the deep pleasure of the engagement:

> Indeed, I often find that a novel, even a well-written and compelling novel, can become a blur to me as soon as I have finished it. I recollect perfectly the feeling of reading it, the mood I occupied, but I am less sure of the narrative details. (84)

The psychologist Mihaly Csikszentmihalyi (1990) would see this experience of reading as an "optimal experience," a form of engagement characterized by effortless control (though our skills as readers seem fully deployed). We experience a lack of self-consciousness, a loss of "normal" time awareness, and a deep pleasure coming from the activity itself. It is "autotelic," an end in itself, a form of immediate gratification, and not a disagreeable or boring effort that will pay off at a later date. It is unalienated labor.

To state my point more axiomatically, *unless we can persuade students that reading is a form of deep, sustained pleasure, they will not choose to read; and because they will not choose to read, they will not develop the skills to make them good readers.*

Recent research on reading comprehension suggests that visualization is critical in helping students enter books and experience this deep pleasure. Good readers are better able to take in details and construct the internal mental theatre of the book. In addition, as Jeff Wilhelm (1997) brilliantly shows, these readers imagine themselves *in* the book; as one of his students remarked, "You gotta *be* the book." Joanne Schooler, a Nancy Drew reader, described her relationship with Nancy Drew as

> understanding her completely, and following her every move, and it was like I was living [right next] to her, but we were separated by this glass wall and I could see and hear everything from her world but she couldn't see or hear anything of mine. And sometimes she would be in danger or ready to make a stupid decision and I was just screaming at her—in my mind I mean—but she couldn't hear me and I was so upset. (58–59)

Joanne has clearly created a virtual reality, a compelling world that she is completely attentive to. Wilhelm goes on to incorporate into his classroom dramatic and artistic opportunities for students to make public the envisioned story space they inhabit as readers. For example, they might create a setting, using puppets or figurines for the characters, to show how they imagine a story unfolds—they also create a puppet for themselves to show where they, as readers, imagine themselves in the story.

Writers, too, speak of a fully visualized world that they create, which often seems to take on a life of its own so that they chronicle as much as create. Here, for example, is what Andre Gide has to say:

> The bad novelist constructs his characters; he directs them and makes them speak. The true novelist listens to them and watches them act; he hears the voices even before he knows them. (In Murray 1990, 102)

Some of the fourth and fifth graders I interviewed described the double perspective they assume when they write. As one described it, it is as if they are writing about a movie that they are in. Here is how one put it:

**SAM:** I imagine that I'm like somewhere in the room and that I'm invisible and I'm watching them do everything and I just think of ideas and put them on paper.

**TN:** So you're not the alien but you're an invisible person in the room watching the alien?

**SAM:** I feel like I'm just watching and they can't see me. They can't say, "Who's that kid in there who's watching us?" And I just realize that they're in there and I'm looking at it but I'm not there.

Anna described an alternate reality, a utopian dreamworld, that she enters when she writes:

**ANNA:** Well, I just think of this happy place that I'm always dreaming of being in and I just feel like my friends are in it and I have no school to go to or stuff. I just like have life freely, like no homework or anything. I really like that place.

**TN:** And is this [story] that place?

**ANNA:** Yeah, same with my other story. I just imagined this fiction place. I go into it and I really got into it.

I would not have guessed the intensity of this identification simply by reading Anna's brief story.

One fourth grader described a similar intense identification with JoJo, a "junk food ant," who turns into Superjojo—"as fast as a slug and as strong as a flea":

**MATT:** Sometimes I feel like I'll write about this little ant called JoJo—a junk food ant—and he goes on these odd adventures and usually gets hurt. So sometimes when I write about him I make him like talking. I feel like I'm in him, like when the Red Sox hit a grand slam and he gets caught on the ball, I feel like I'm flying through space like this. (*He leans back in his chair and mimes holding onto the ball.*)

**TN:** So when you're writing you feel like you're in the air?

**Matt:** Yeah when he gets hurt in the air, and I'm kind of like up there. I'm JoJo.

I think it's significant that Matt leaned back in his chair to show his physical involvement with JoJo. He may have provided an answer to the objections I have noted in this chapter, for his writing process is not purely mental activity. He, and others I interviewed, feel physically "there" in their writing, and they act in concert with the characters they created.

Few areas of education have been studied as relentlessly as reading. A regular research industry has been at work for almost a century, and one might imagine the reading act to be transparently exposed by now. Yet for many readers, and particularly boys, the attraction of sustained silent reading is baffling. Nonreaders see it as a form of isolation that runs counter to every social instinct they possess. It calls for unimaginable disciplining of the body; consequently it is the perfect tool for a school system that must keep students still. Exhortations that equate reading with job success, civic duty, or cultural patriotism are not likely to be convincing in the long run (or even short run). The transformation will not come from dubious elitist claims that a certain type of "serious" reading will make us better, more sensitive people.

Instead, the habit of reading comes from the desire to enter and reenter a state of attention, from the pleasure we gain in encounters with characters and storytellers who become as real, sometimes more real, than actual people we know. It does not have to be a lonely act.

But our ability to engage students in this deeply involved reading and writing is compromised by often unspoken class and gender biases—ones that define the kind of story that can make it into the classroom and the kind that must stay outside. It is to these questions of taste and distaste that we now turn.

# CHAPTER FOUR

# Taste and Distaste

Trashy and positively unwholesome literature is
so widely extended throughout the country . . . [that]
persons who read little or nothing beside trashy
novels of the day would be better not to read at all. . . .
The most popular and best thumbed works in any
reading rooms are invariably those that are the most
worthless—we might say the most dangerous.
—Egerton Ryerson, influential Canadian educator, 1870

A couple of years ago, I met a friend, author Carolyn
Coman, at a swimming lake near campus. Carolyn's
most recent book, *What Jamie Saw*, had recently been a finalist for
the Newbery Award, and after years of work her career was finally
taking off. Her son David, a middle schooler, was also there, drift-
ing nearby on a float as we talked. Carolyn mentioned that one of
her next projects was to write a book that David *might actually
choose to read*, a fantasy story that would move more quickly than
her earlier books.

As she was talking, David looked skeptically at his award-winning mother and said, "Yeah, I don't want fifty pages about the next five minutes of your life."

"Promise, David. I promise."

Studies of boys' preferences in reading confirm David's bias in favor of action over character development and introspection. According to British researcher Elaine Millard, boys who do read prefer stories that "emphasize action over personal relationships, excitement over the unfolding of character, and humor most of all" (1997, 61). She adds that these preferences put boys at odds with literature typically chosen for study in schools.

In this chapter we will switch from quantitative measures of gender difference to a more qualitative exploration of boys' narrative preferences. I will argue that all narratives are not created (or treated) equally. Boys' traditional favorites—information books, humor, science fiction, and action stories—are often treated as subliterature, something that a reader should move beyond as he moves toward realistic fiction with thematic weight (to David's "five minutes in fifty pages"). In fact, some of the literature boys enjoy (and produce) might not even be thought to deserve that name. Take one of my son's (and my own) favorite genres, tables of team standings. This one (Figure 4–1) appeared on April 15, 2002, as the National Basketball Association season approaches the playoffs. This is not merely raw information. Not some transactional bit of data. For the skilled reader this table is full of stores, even morality tales, though it takes a bit of prior knowledge to construct them.

We see, for example, what is probably the sad conclusion of Michael Jordan's second comeback, with his Washington team well out of contention. We also see the gratifying emergence (at least for Boston fans) of the Celtics after years of mediocrity; they not only are *in* the playoffs, but begin with home court advantage. But what jumps out is the striking disparity of the two conferences, with *four* teams in the West having better records than the East winner, New Jersey—and Sacramento finishing with an eleven-game winning streak. Is this the year for them to dislodge the

| EASTERN CONFERENCE | | | | | | | |
|---|---|---|---|---|---|---|---|
| | W | L | Pct. | GB | Streak | Home | Away | Conf. |
| 1. c-N.J. .........51 | 29 | .638 | — | L 1 | 33-7 | 18-22 | 34-18 |
| 2. c-Detroit ....48 | 32 | .600 | 3 | W 1 | 25-15 | 23-17 | 36-16 |
| 3. p-BOST. .....47 | 33 | .588 | 4 | W 2 | 26-14 | 21-19 | 34-19 |
| 4. p-Orlando ..43 | 37 | .538 | 8 | L 3 | 27-13 | 16-24 | 28-24 |
| 6. p-Phila. ......43 | 37 | .538 | 8 | W 2 | 22-18 | 21-19 | 31-21 |
| 5. p-Charl. .....42 | 38 | .525 | 9 | L 1 | 20-20 | 22-18 | 29-23 |
| 7. Toronto ....41 | 39 | .513 | 10 | W 2 | 23-17 | 18-22 | 28-24 |
| 8. Milw. .........40 | 40 | .500 | 11 | W 1 | 24-16 | 16-24 | 28-24 |
| 9. Indiana .....40 | 40 | .500 | 11 | W 3 | 24-16 | 16-24 | 25-27 |
| 10. Wash. ........36 | 45 | .444 | 15½ | L 2 | 21-19 | 15-26 | 24-29 |
| 11. *Miami ......35 | 44 | .443 | 15½ | W 1 | 18-21 | 17-23 | 21-30 |
| 12. Atlanta ......33 | 47 | .413 | 18 | W 1 | 23-17 | 10-30 | 21-31 |
| 13. *New York .29 | 50 | .367 | 21½ | L 4 | 19-21 | 10-29 | 19-32 |
| 14. Cleve. ........29 | 51 | .363 | 22 | L 2 | 20-20 | 9-31 | 20-32 |
| 15. Chicago .....20 | 60 | .250 | 31 | L 1 | 14-27 | 6-33 | 12-40 |

| WESTERN CONFERENCE | | | | | | | |
|---|---|---|---|---|---|---|---|
| | W | L | Pct. | GB | Streak | Home | Away | Conf. |
| 1. *p-Sacra. ...60 | 19 | .759 | — | W 11 | 35-4 | 25-15 | 36-13 |
| 2. p-San Ant. .56 | 24 | .700 | 4½ | W 7 | 31-9 | 25-15 | 36-14 |
| 3. p-Lakers ...56 | 24 | .700 | 4½ | L 1 | 32-7 | 24-17 | 35-15 |
| 4. *p-Dallas ...55 | 24 | .696 | 5 | W 1 | 29-11 | 26-13 | 32-17 |
| 5. p-Minn. ......49 | 31 | .613 | 11½ | W 1 | 28-11 | 21-20 | 28-23 |
| 6. p-Port. .......48 | 33 | .593 | 13 | W 2 | 29-11 | 19-22 | 26-25 |
| 7. p-Seattle ...44 | 36 | .550 | 16½ | L 2 | 25-15 | 19-21 | 25-25 |
| 8. p-Utah .......44 | 36 | .550 | 16½ | W 2 | 25-15 | 19-21 | 25-25 |
| 9. Clippers .....38 | 42 | .475 | 22½ | L 3 | 24-15 | 14-27 | 22-28 |
| 10. Phoenix .....35 | 45 | .438 | 25½ | L 2 | 22-18 | 13-27 | 23-27 |
| 11. *Houston ...28 | 51 | .354 | 32 | L 1 | 18-22 | 10-29 | 18-32 |
| 12. Denver .......26 | 54 | .325 | 34½ | W 2 | 19-21 | 7-33 | 18-32 |
| 13. *Memphis .22 | 57 | .278 | 38 | L 1 | 15-26 | 7-31 | 13-36 |
| 14. Gold. St. .....20 | 60 | .250 | 40½ | L 5 | 13-27 | 7-33 | 12-38 |

c — clinched division title    p — clinched playoff spot
* — not including late game

FIGURE 4–1  *NBA Standings, Box Scores*

Lakers? And then there are the poor Bulls, Jordan's old team, winners of only six games on the road. And so on. The dynastic stories, the rises and falls. It's all there in the literature of sports tables.

But it is far too common—and too simplistic—to divide language into two classes, the aesthetic and the transactional. The aesthetic, typically narrative fiction and poetry, fulfills a human need for stories and the insights they give into our experience; the transactional, usually persuasive or informational writing, is brutely functional, helping us carry on the business of the world (see, for example, Britton et al. 1976 and Rosenblatt 1978). Yet facts can have a romance all their own. Learning that a dinosaur was 90 feet long is more than the simple addition of "information"; it is an evocative stimulus to imagination (picture that tail!). Learning that the oxygen content on top of Mt. Everest is one-third that at sea level helps us to imagine the gasping for breath that occurs near the top. And for many boys, nowhere is this romance with facts more evident, more persistent, than in the "literature" of sports, the drama of lists. (It may also explain the early comfort many boys feel with mathematics; they've dealt with decimals—batting averages—even before they knew what decimals were.)

My son created his most prized literary artifact in middle school, an elaborate set of statistical tables and records of an imaginary basketball league. It included a page on the stadiums of the teams; this on the arena for the Buffalo team:

Buffalo Blizzard
The Warm Spot
Capacity: 12,018
Average Attendance: 11,924
Site: Buffalo, NY

He placed himself on the New England Storm (which played in the Shelter Dome) and listed his height as 6'11". For each of the six teams, he rated each player on four categories: Speed, Shot, Aggressive, and Smarts. For the Blizzard the ratings were as follows:

|            |     |        | Speed | Shot | Aggressive | Smarts |
|------------|-----|--------|-------|------|------------|--------|
| Matt Young | G   | 6'2"   | 9     | 9    | 9          | 9      |
| Neil Smith | F   | 6'5"   | 9     | 9    | 9          | 9      |
| Sam Jones  | C   | 6'10"  | 8     | 10   | 9          | 8      |
| Bill Smith | C-F | 6'9"   | 7     | 8    | 9          | 7      |

In his bedroom, he would play out games to fifty points with a miniature Nerf basketball, announcing the game as he went. As he played he claims he kept in mind the performance rating for each player; for example, Blizzard center-forward Bill Smith, lacking a bit in "Smarts," might commit a mental mistake at a crucial part of the game. Andy recorded the result of each game, including the length *to the second*. He also kept running team standings for the duration of the league, from April 13 to May 15.

To look at these tables and statistics, it would be hard to imag-ine that they had emotional weight at all. They appear to be noth-ing more than sterile lists, yet for my son they were—and remain—extraordinarily evocative. There is no easy one-for-one equivalence between direct expression of emotion and the actual emotional investment of the writer (and reader). When boys' writ-ing is read as resolutely "impersonal," I suspect there is a form of literalism going on: The emotion isn't named, so it must not exist. Because we could not imagine ourselves emotionally involved with the writing, we assume that the writer couldn't be involved either.

Even when boys write narrative fiction, they often fail to pro-duce the kind of work that meets the aesthetic criteria of some educators. Critics of boys' story writing claim that it typically has "pace and event at the expense of everything else" (Peter Thomas, quoted in Barrs 2000, 289). British gender researcher Myra Barrs, drawing on the work of Britton, defines interiority almost exclu-sively as retrospective, a reflection on a prior event or experience, a high-level form of "gossip."

> It is through such informal, gossipy talk that we explore our responses and reactions to life experiences, and such talk is also our medium for exploring responses to, and understandings of, texts (media or literary). Through refining these responses, we learn to be more thoughtful, subtle, and discriminating readers. (2000, 289)

In other words, this form of responding to texts, through gossip-like reflection, is not merely one means of response, it is the true goal of reading. Barrs argues that this form of retrospection char-acterizes literacy at its most profound level. We should therefore not be seeking out alternative literacies (ones more congenial to boys). Rather than "agitating about boys' underachievement" Barrs claims we need to help boys develop in areas (particularly characterization) where girls are typically stronger.

In my experience, encouraging boys to make their characters more lifelike and realistic—and more reflective—is invariably met with resistance. The adventure genre they are working in allows little space for retrospection. The mental action is pointed ahead. If we think of the *Star Wars* trilogy, much of the dialogue focuses on planning. Constantly at risk, the central question is not "how am I responding to this," but "what must I do?" And even that reflection must be subordinated to the primary action of the story.

I'm arguing, then, that some types of literate activity are barely recognized as such—and have no place in schools. Other types become the primary evidence of school literacy. Not only is the "good reader" a fiction reader, but she is one who reads a particular type of fiction—in a particular way. In fact, many students who classify themselves as nonreaders read quite a lot; they see themselves as nonreaders because they don't read extended works of fiction. (Smith and Wilhelm [2002] document how "length" is a primary deterrent for boys.)

In her 1997 study of junior high girls, Margaret Finders interviewed one working-class mother and found the same form of self-denigration. She admitted to reading "books" but not "book-books." Intrigued, Finders asked her to explain the distinction:

> Books were what she read—magazines and information to beautify her home. This reading consisted of cookbooks, home decorating guides, and magazines. "Book-books" designated those things she did not read. They were, in her words, "what you were supposed to read in school. What you have to read in school. I wasn't very good at it. You know, *long* novels." (92)

She is not a "good reader." Her focused, pragmatic reading in the areas of her primary interest, home improvement, doesn't really count—evidence of the triumph of literature in the twentieth-century curriculum. I suspect that her reading involves something more than pragmatic "information"; it may involve an imaginary entry into an alternative way of living that she could only approximate.

## Hierarchies of Literary Experience

Not all stories, not even all "book-books," are created equal, or at least treated equally in schools. Our students are awash in narratives—they are dexterous channel surfers able to keep two or three stories alive simultaneously. It is little wonder that those who teach might choose to make a stand for a *type* of morally serious narrative, call it *literature*, that we like to claim makes greater demands and offers greater rewards. Like any bias, this one can seem like nothing more than a simple recognition of demonstrable literary merit: Some literature has the power to challenge and change us for the better; the more popular literature can amuse and entertain us but nothing more. Judith Langer ends her book *Envisioning Literature* (1995) with this ringing claim:

> Literature makes us better thinkers. It moves us to see the multi-sidedness of situations and therefore expands the breadth of our visions, moving us to dreams and solutions that might not be otherwise imagined. It affects how we go about learning in academic situations, how we solve problems at work and at home. And it moves us to consider our interconnectedness with others and the intrinsic pluralness of meaning; it helps us become more human. (145)

Langer places great emphasis on the moral functionalism of literature, the extent to which it assists readers in becoming more sensitive, more tolerant, more socially effective human beings. Her last sentence is missing the comparative term—"more human" than what? We might guess she is claiming that reading literature helps us become more human than *we would be if we didn't read in this way*. But it could also be read as more human *than those who don't read in this way*, those in an equivalent state to the unimproved selves we would be if we didn't read. According to Langer, reading creates an expansive awareness of "others" that those locked into particular social groups cannot attain. In other words, reading has a special capacity for creating ethical sensitivity; it is more powerful than other, more popular art forms (rap, music video, stand-up comedy); it is even more effective than *actual* social interaction with others, such as working at a convenience store.

The fact that this rationale rests so strongly on moral efficacy suggest an uneasiness with claiming *pleasure* as the end of reading. The intense, trancelike state of immersion in a book or story is not enough. This moralism may be a carryover from an older reading tradition in this country, evident in the McGuffey readers, that used school narrative to stress civic or ethical lessons. After all, how could the enterprise of English teaching, which rests so profoundly on literature, be justified by the deep pleasure we gain from reading? It seems hedonistic. By emphasizing the humanizing function of literature, Langer gives it a reassuring place in the curriculum. It can be a corrective to antisocial or disruptive or amoral tendencies traditionally associated with adolescents. Books can be instruments of socialization.

Langer is clearly not advocating a return to this didacticism, but her claim bears traces of that tradition. One essential feature of this literary "envisionment," as she describes it, is the necessity of discussions; the experience of reading is not sufficient and must be supplemented by discussion, sharing, and analysis of the various "text worlds" students create. The sheer performance of a book is not enough and must be supplemented by a form of analysis.

I have not given Langer's position this attention to deny the value of the literary experiences she advocates; in fact, her emphasis on visualization of plot provided a key element of the pleasure good readers experience (Keene and Zimmerman 1997). Instead, I want to look at what her view leaves out. Not all literature can produce (or even attempts to produce) the moral sensitivity Langer sees as the end of literary study. This claim may hold for *Beloved*, but not for *Pet Sematary*. In fact, some genres, particularly parody, satirize this regime of seriousness. Humor is performative and resists "discussion," though it invites reenactment and resavoring. Some texts promiscuously give up their virtue so easily that discussion is not needed.

The French sociologist Pierre Bourdieu also raises questions about the claim that a particular type of literary experience leads to "fuller, more thoughtful, and more informed members of the world—in both life and literature" (1984, 8). Again, more than whom? Bourdieu would claim that the unnamed "other" is the mass of people not identified with an educated class. One characteristic of this more popular aesthetic is the desire to wholeheartedly enter into a fictional world:

> The desire to enter into the game, identifying with the characters' joys and sufferings, worrying about their fate, espousing their hopes and ideals, living their life, is based on a form of *investment*, a sort of deliberate "naivety," ingenuousness, good-natured credulity (We're here to enjoy ourselves). (33)

From this standpoint, any perceived obscurity or complexity or artfulness (things that might be "discussed") may get in the way of this involvement. When students complain that certain texts are "analyzed to death," they may be affirming their loyalty to this more "naive" form of reading.

But it is mistaken to see this stance as resistant to any social message. In fact, much popular entertainment mocks the attitudes and pretenses of those who have power over us. According to Bourdieu, this counteraesthetic glorifies a form of expressiveness that might be looked down upon as sentimental or sensationalist; it embraces a form of spectacle that might appear gaudy. Rather than fostering individual sensitivity, it invites a surrender to collective enthusiasm. Using the circus and melodrama as examples of significant working-class pleasures, he writes:

> Through collective festivity they give rise to an array of spectacular delights (I'm thinking of the music-hall sets, light opera, or big feature film)—fabulous sets, glittering costumes, exciting music, lively action, enthusiastic actors—like all forms of the comic and

especially those working through satire and parody of the "great,"
they satisfy the taste for and sense of revelry, the plain speaking and
hearty laughter which liberate by setting the social world head over
heels, overturning conventions and proprieties. (34)

Professional wrestling fits this description well with its gaudiness,
violence, bodily display, and mockery of political correctness. This
entertainment, according to Bourdieu, does not function as a civilizing agent, helping to create better world citizens. Rather, it
turns the world upside down, mocking those in authority (teachers, judges, politicians, parents, referees) whose job it is to monitor and evaluate our behavior. Bourdieu's analysis also suggests a
literary hierarchy turned upside down, with parody and satire, so
beloved by boys, being the central genres of resistance.

The claim for the special moral power of quality literature is
so regularly cited that it may be hopeless to raise questions about
it. But as I write this, fires still smoulder at the World Trade Center, and the bodies of hundreds of dead firemen and policemen are
yet to be recovered. It seems to me unlikely that literary sensibility played much of a role in their acts of exemplary courage. More
likely, they acted out of an uncompromising sense of duty that
lacked the nuance of any literary representation. This kind of
moral code comes from immersion in a culture where mandates
are either unspoken or articulated in brief aphorisms: "We go into
the building when everyone else is leaving." Those with highly literate sensibilities often treat the aphorisms of daily moral action
as unthinking simplistic clichés; they are embarrassing signs that
the individual cannot move beyond given collective wisdom and
think for himself. Yet a saying like "When the going gets tough,
the tough get going" will always have moral and motivational
utility—and even the highly educated turn to this popular code
in times of difficulty. I am not criticizing literature that seeks to
engage serious issues of race, identity, family dysfunction, and ethical responsibilities. I am not arguing against books that depict the
inner states, the subjective lives of the characters ("five minutes in
fifty pages"). This is the literature I regularly choose to read

myself—but not because I think it makes me a better person. It is one type of literature I want to see in schools and classrooms.

Rather, I am challenging the claims made for this literature and the implicit (or explicit) moral hierarchy that sets this type of reading *above* more popular forms of literary activity. These hierarchies work to rationalize social class divisions; a certain "taste" marks the reader as having greater sensitivity and refinement of judgment. One's economic privilege, then, comes not from an accident of birth or inequitable social policies, but from one's perceived sensitivity and refinement, one's superior moral discernment. In Bourdieu's terms, this taste for seriousness confers "social capital" to a class of readers, setting them apart from those who read for plot or escape (and from those who do not read at all). One thing that an elite education in fact teaches is how to construct a hierarchical map of reading; it helps develop a "taste" for the serious and a "distaste" for the vulgar ("popular," in its original meaning). It is also a map that places most of the genres boys love near the bottom.

## Realism and Nostalgia

If all published literature is not created equal, the same could be said for student writing. The grounds for distinctions are rooted in concerns about how consumerism and mass culture are redefining childhood. While one of the goals of the writing process movement in the 1980s was to open up the range of choices available to students, there were usually implicit criteria about what constituted a "good choice" or a "good topic." Thinking back to the early days of Donald Graves' groundbreaking study of children's writing, I recall one piece of writing, "Old Birch," that was endlessly read at conferences, often provoking tears from the audience. Written by a third grader, it described in effective detail a large birch tree in her back yard, the place it had in her life, the sadness she felt at its being cut down, and her vow to keep it alive in memory (and, obviously, her writing). I suspect we were all impressed by her intense, almost precocious feeling for the natural world. There was something ideologically *right* about it; it resonated with a set of largely hidden values we brought to the reading. But to be clear about this ideology seemed at that time to be a violation of the promise to open up topic choice; it would suggest a hidden agenda—and of course there *was* a hidden agenda. None of us could escape the pattern of our own gratifications. None of us checked our literary preferences at the door. It's that agenda, that implicit sense of taste, that I want to probe.

The expression "good choice" is an oxymoron, with the two terms in considerable tension. "Choice" implies a form of freedom to go outside the range of the conventional and appropriate; yet the "good" reins it in, establishing a boundary within which choices must be made in order to qualify as "good." Progressive educators like Graves (and Jean-Jacques Rousseau) want to avoid external coercion, which students will resist or hollowly obey (and which will make the method appear authoritarian); yet they clearly must set boundaries within which choice must be made. The solution is to win students over to a particular standard of taste that coincides with the standards of the teacher and program. As Rousseau candidly admitted, "[Emile] ought to do only what he wants; but he ought to want only what you want him to do" ([1762] 1979, 120). A tricky business, this—to make claims both for student volition *and* for a particular standard of writing achievement.

We can begin to construct the ideology underlying the criteria for "good choice" by looking at some of the advice Graves and others have offered to teachers. Here is Graves on topic choice:

> The exercise of judgment in choosing topics takes time. At first, children may write about last night's stale TV plot, or the same topic for six successive writings. This is where it begins, but not where it ends. (1983, 31)

Children, Graves argues, should be encouraged to search their lives and interests for compelling topics like Debby Nichols'

"Old Birch." He presents a list of "good topics" that children in his study chose, and dominating this list are hobbies, pets, and relationships with family. Television was generally perceived as a distraction from the core of life experience that the student should be exploring. In fact, fictional plots of any kind were virtually dismissed in the early descriptions of this pedagogy. The mantra was "write about what you know and care about." In other words, write nonfiction.

We can see the same scale of values at work in an episode described in Lucy Calkins' *Living Between the Lines* (1991). She describes an exchange between Shelley Harwayne and a student struggling to find a topic:

> When Shelley Harwayne . . . drew a chair alongside Ipolito Diaz's desk, the boy sighed deeply. "I don't have anything to write about," he said. "Nothing happens in my life. All I do is watch TV, feed the pigeons, watch TV, feed the pigeons."
>
> "Is one of these topics especially important?" Shelley asked.
>
> "Well," Ipolito answered, "I suppose feeding the pigeons is more important because if I don't feed them they'll starve." (34)

Harwayne then works with Ipolito to develop this topic, a decision I suspect almost any teacher would agree with. Yet the conversation could have gone differently: Harwayne could have asked Ipolito to talk about his experience as a TV watcher and perhaps create a version of one of his favorite shows. If the topic of feeding pigeons is so much more promising, why is that? Why is the TV topic so unpromising? What scale of valuation causes a teacher to lean one way rather than the other? What desire or anxiety on the part of the reader does the pigeon topic address?

The desire for certain types of experiential writing may be part of a broader cultural concern for the disappearance of local culture and the loss of a childhood rooted in that local culture. Calkins powerfully illustrates this longing for a threatened, perhaps vanishing, version of childhood. Near the beginning of *Living Between the Lines*, she invites the reader to consider a photograph.

Now we realize that the reason to invite children's lives into the classroom has less to do with finding topics for writing than the fact that we cannot learn unless we are alive to our existence. Above her writing desk, Annie Dillard has a photograph that might be hung above every classroom door. The photograph is of a little Amazonian boy whose face is sticking out of river rapids. White water is pounding all around his head and his dark eyes are looking up. "The little boy is completely alive," Dillard says. "He's letting the mystery of existence beat on him. He's having a childhood, and I think he knows it. And I think he will come out of the water strong, and ready to do some good." (13)

One way to analyze this powerful image and the effect it has on Dillard (and presumably Calkins), is to make substitutions. Would it work as well if the rapt form of experience was a child's absorption in a video game? It's unlikely. The photograph shows the child (Rousseau's *natural* preindustrial child) immersed, literally, in an environment untouched by modern technology. In fact, a picture of a child immersed in a video game would be viewed not as an "experience" at all, but as simply "virtual" living.

Equally interesting is the projection of cultural anxiety that is going on. Dillard claims the boy knows "he is having a childhood," but one wonders if such a question would ever occur to the boy. The "loss of childhood" has been a concern of Western progressive educators since the time of Rousseau and Wordsworth (for more recent versions, see Elkind 1981 and Postman 1982). But is "having a childhood" an issue among Amazonians?

By naming this cultural anxiety, I believe, Calkins comes closest to explaining why the writing process/workshop movement has shown a consistent preference for autobiographical writing that represents nontechnological forms of experience. In effect, teachers can help children claim a childhood through the act of writing, through shaping and reliving experiences with grandparents, parents, siblings, hobbies, and pets (which are themselves reminders of an earlier, rural existence). When writing about these topics, children place themselves not as consumers or TV watchers, but as caretakers—they assume the morally reassuring roles of stewards (e.g., Ipolito tending his pigeons).

I became aware of the deep attraction of this construction when I spent a week as a teacher in residence at a Hawaiian elementary school. My plan was to share a piece of nature writing that I did—about Durham, New Hampshire's Oyster River in winter—and ask them to write about a place they especially liked. This being Hawaii, I imagined them writing about some *natural* place, a beach, a rain forest, an active volcano. But even after I'd read my description, they picked theme parks, indoor amusement arcades, and water slides—the kind of places children *anywhere* could pick. The boys were enthralled with monster trucks crushing rows of cars. My first reaction (besides feeling foolish) was to think that it was such a loss for them to miss out on what made Hawaii so special (at least to an adult outsider). Then, slowly, it occurred to me that I was hoping they would act as *natives*, as locals, as children somehow uncontaminated by mass culture, as a human wilderness preserve. My construction did not match theirs; like children in Durham, they chose the popular culture venues that fed their fantasies of power.

The bias against television as a legitimate source of writing topics is grounded in the American social-class system. While all sectors of the population watch television, the professional middle and upper classes take pains to minimize that fact. Often no television is visible in the main living room, suggesting that other cultural and social activities (e.g., listening to music, conversation) are more highly valued, more representative of the lifestyle. The same statement is made in upscale hotel rooms, where the television, while available, is often kept hidden behind wooden console doors. At the Ritz, one may open these doors and *choose* to watch television; at Motel 6, where the TV is in plain view, one is *expected* to watch. To make the TV too blatantly visible is to admit a lack of balance in one's cultural diet, and the professional who admits to watching often does so apologetically, as if acknowledging a momentary lapse or a special decision to watch a particularly worthwhile show. In other words, it's not a *habit*. Bourdieu might argue that this *attitude* toward television watching is a form of cultural capital, serving as a marker of membership in a professional social class.

Statistics on television watching show extraordinary racial differences. Between the ages of eight and eighteen, the average white child spends 2 hours, 47 minutes per day watching television; the average black child spends 4 hours, 41 minutes; and the average Hispanic child, 3 hours, 50 minutes (Rideout 2000). The average black child spends *almost two hours per day more* than the average white child in TV watching; the average Hispanic child spends almost an hour more. The reasons for these differentials are complex, and undoubtedly rooted in the general economic advantage among whites that allows for tighter supervision and a wider range of activities (various types of lessons, camps, book reading). For Hispanic and black children, then, TV watching accounts for a more significant (at least numerically) form of cultural experience.

If the predominant attitude of schools is to discount the potential value of this TV watching (to wean them from "stale" TV plots), the end result may be, as Anne Dyson argues, to cut them off from the most powerful and pervasive narrative forms they know. If schools make no place for the cultural material that children find meaningful, they "risk reinforcing societal divisions in children's orientations to each other, to cultural art forms, and to school itself" (1997, 181).

I am arguing that the professional middle and upper-middle class, to which most teachers belong, sets up a hierarchy of cultural experience—and that TV watching is near the bottom of that hierarchy. Most TV is viewed as mere mind candy, as escape, as an evasion of living itself. Or it is viewed as a pernicious cultural force that promotes consumerism, sexism, short attention spans, and a love of cheap thrills. This attitude can serve to systematically disadvantage minority groups, for whom TV is the primary source of entertainment. The question Dyson asks—and it's a good one—is why literacy teachers cannot treat television as a resource. Given the extraordinary gap between minority and white literacy achievement (most extreme for African American boys), shouldn't schools make every effort to build upon existing narrative preferences?

Graves modified his position on fiction after the 1983 publication of his main text, *Writing: Teachers and Children at Work* (see, for example, *Experiment with Fiction* [1989]), but even this new advocacy mirrors a general discomfort with nonrealistic fiction. He takes a developmental approach with the earlier, less-mature writing that's characterized by implausible action sequences (often violent) and "generic" characters. Character development becomes the index of growth—and, consequently, the main line of instruction. In other words, Graves views this less-mature writing as lacking the traits of more developed realistic fiction—rather than as demonstrating students' allegiance to nonrealistic genres. A comic book, after all, is not an undeveloped short story; it is a distinctive genre with its own rules.

To a degree, Graves' push for characterization is relevant to all genres. Even the creators of Marvel Comics heroes like Spiderman stress the need for human traits and motivations (Daniels 1991). I suspect that teachers prefer realism for at least two reasons. First, students are moving toward kinds of writing we voluntarily read (we don't have to *pretend*). Second, realistic fiction depends on the intense observation of lived experience, attention to relationships, language, physical appearance, and personal reactions and judgments. Like good autobiographical writing, it pushes the writer to create a distinctive, particularized world, and this effort is self-actualizing. To go back to the Amazonian photograph, the writer can claim a fully experienced existence. By contrast, the space adventure or the comic book does not require this attentiveness.

Elaine Millard argues that there are flaws in this developmental model because it fails to acknowledge the powerful appeal of what she calls "symbolic narratives," which may feature battles between forces of good and evil (for example, the *Star Wars* trilogy). These narratives often appear formulaic and overly schematic to highly literate adults, but according to Millard they have the psychological power of oral folklore. This comment refers specifically to reading, but it is relevant to writing as well:

> It is too easy . . . to think of these more symbolic narratives as an
> earlier stage of reading and consider the psychological focus of the
> realistic novel, with its emphasis on the exploration of "character,"
> a more mature form of writing. To set against this, we can argue
> that there is something perhaps as potent as character in the
> unravelling of a good plot, which partakes of the nature of oral
> storytelling. (1997, 110)

The power and memorability of such stories comes from their
"chaste compactness which precludes psychological analysis"
(Benjamin, quoted in Millard 1997, 110).

Space stories are one male genre that is tolerated but not usually enjoyed by teachers—because they seem so devoid of characterization or interior action. Boys seem to perseverate in this genre,
adding adventure upon adventure almost without even a gesture
toward characterization. Bradley, a fourth grader in my study, had
written such a story, or so I thought. It began:

> Optimas flew over out of the hatch and Megatron and their teams
> were close behind. They were trying to get to a mountain full of
> energon. The Predicons can use the stable energon to make them
> more powerful.

The story continues with pitched battles and attempts to locate
hidden energy sources that allow for major transformations. It was
for me devoid of characters and hard to follow, a takeoff on trans-
former games and video games. Drawing on the research of Jeff
Wilhelm (1997) I asked Bradley "where he was" when he was writing the story. Was he at his desk? In the story itself? Was he an
actor or a watcher?

It seemed to me an abstract question for a fourth grader, but
it made immediate sense to Bradley:

> When I write a story I sometimes get into it so much that
> I actually feel it is happening. I write as fast as I can to get
> all of my thoughts down because it feels as if it is really

happening and that you're really in a war, and you have to think fast and be careful—the leaders—so you don't get any of your troops in danger.

Bradley seems to describe two forms of involvement: He is both an observer and an actor in the mental movie that he is creating. He leads—and chronicles his leadership. One of his classmates described this same doubleness: "It's kind of like watching a movie and you're in it." In other words, it is dangerous to *presume* a lack of investment by the writers simply because we as readers as not invested.

My point here is to argue not against realistic fiction, but against a model (or simply a bias) that sets it as the culmination of writing development. One of my college students describes his own brutal encounter with this bias, which years later still rankles him:

> I wrote short, comic book novellas, I suppose you would call them, and turned them into my Advanced Writing teacher my senior year of high school. "Despise" would be an understatement to describe what he felt toward them. A supporter of Conrad, Hemingway, and Dickens, and other classic writers, he wasn't familiar with comic books beyond what he picked up as a child. He said something that I've been an opponent of my entire time writing, the ever-popular, "Write what you know. Anything else you're just taking what you have seen on TV or read in a book somewhere else. That's not you. That's someone else's view of the topic at hand. Write what you know." If people only wrote what they knew, science fiction, horror fiction, amongst other lines of best-selling books, would never be created.

While I'm sure this teacher saw his speech as one that might liberate Kevin to examine the particularity of his own experience, Kevin saw it as elitist and simply ignorant.

In my interviews with third, fourth, and fifth graders, another rationale came forward from both boys and girls. Real-life experience seemed to them not so much something to represent as it was something to transcend. Fiction allowed them to claim power and privileges they could never claim in "real life"; as one third grader put it, "my imagination is bigger than my life"—and presumably better. Sometimes fiction allowed them the transgressive pleasure of "being bad." In fifth grader Sarah's story, she makes herself part of Carmen Sandiego's gang that has stolen the Statue of Liberty:

SARAH: I'm part of Carmen's gang. I'm really bad.
TN: Why do you make yourself really bad?
SARAH: I like being bad. It's kind of cool. You can do all of this bad stuff and not get in trouble for it. *I* stole the Statue of Liberty. Like in real life you can do something but you can get in trouble, but in a story you can do whatever you want. You can jump off a roof if you want.
TN: So you could steal something and get away with it?
SARAH: Yeah, kind of funny. But it's not like when people write stories like this they're like that in real life. They just wish they could do it. I guess.

I suspect those interested in the craft of fiction would wince at the claim that in fiction "you can do whatever you want." But the students I interviewed treated fiction writing as a free utopian space where they could act out, claiming power or skill that they didn't possess in "real life." I asked one fourth-grade boy why he preferred to write fiction about sports teams when he could choose to write nonfiction accounts of his own games. He responded, "Probably because if I made it up I could be better than I really am."

Karen's story, "The Case of the Missing Bill Russell," is a more extended example of how students use fiction to improve on life experience. Her story takes place in Disney World, where ex-Celtic great Bill Russell is kidnapped by Mr. Creep when Russell's companion, Larry Bird, is playing with Karen at Splash Mountain. Modeling her story on a clue sequence in a mystery she read, *The Eleventh Hour* (Base 1993), Karen has Mr. Creep leave a series of rhyming clues that take her through Disney World to A Small World After All, where they find Bill Russell playing with a kid from Poland while being forced to repeatedly sing "It's a Small World After All" (now *there's* an image). The story is a wonderful example of the dreamlike quality of much student fiction, where multiple worlds—friendship groups, sports affiliations, literature, song, and lived experience—are fused, a process Dyson refers to as "hybridization" (1999).

During the interview with Karen, I asked if she had recently been to Disney World. She had of course been there, and the differences between her fictional movement through the park and her actual experience were dramatic:

> I didn't actually get to go on Thunder Mountain and Space Mountain [as she did in her story] because it was too crowded on Space Mountain, with big humongous lines. It's like all the kids in the school lined up. Big lines, and we had to wait. And my sister was too young to go on the ride and we couldn't, and there was this age limit, and again she was too young for that.

Although Karen had still found her trip enjoyable, in her fiction she could jettison her younger sister and her family, substitute her friends, include players from her favorite basketball team, and move through the park as if there were no lines or restrictions.

## Versions of Power

In this chapter I have tried to sketch two very different versions of student empowerment through reading and writing. The key word for one might be "authenticity," for the other, "power." One promotes a highly particularized attentiveness to personal experience (including the vicarious encounters made in reading) and the self-actualization that comes from such experience. The other works more with generic, communal genres (such as space stories) in which writers find ways to assume power—or to mock power. One tends to view popular media, particularly television and video culture, as an impediment to authentic living, a pallid commercialized substitute for the kinds of experiences that can make students more sensitive and ethical citizens of the world. The other finds, in that same commercialized media, narratives of power and resistance that when appropriated by the writer can offer a sense of control. The noted literacy educator Mike Rose (1989), for example, describes his own feeling of powerlessness growing up in a poor section of Los Angeles. Warned by his teachers that comic books were "bad for him," he persisted in reading them, drawing strength from the "virtuous omnipotence" of the heroes (224).

I have been critical of certain formulations of the writing process and writing workshop approaches, not because they have a particular agenda, but because they fail to make that agenda clear. When terms like "authentic" are used, institutional power and class bias are erased from the picture. The actions of literacy instruction are portrayed as entirely benign and self-evidently beneficial to the students. The value of a "literature-based curriculum" or "topic choice" becomes almost inarguable, because they are designed to meet individual "needs." We are not, then, promoting an agenda; we are not exercising power. We are not imposing taste.

But a number of literacy researchers have shown that seemingly self-evident, benign, "normal" school practices can be quietly discriminating. In one of the most significant essays ever written on writing instruction, Lisa Delpit (1988) reminds middle-class educators of disjunctions between their assumptions about learning and the values of those they teach. She deftly noted that even the tendency to use indirect requests (e.g., "It's getting noisy in here" equals "Quiet down") may be mystifying to some African American children. Similarly, Shirley Brice Heath (1983) shows that typical school "display questions"—where the child answers a question even though the teacher knows the answer—are far more familiar to what she calls "mainstream" economic groups than to the less economically advantaged groups she studied.

Both remind us that even the most "natural" practices spring from class-bound (and race-bound) social language practices that may appear arbitrary to those outside the mainstream culture. I have tried to extend this argument to examine the often unstated aesthetic hierarchy in reading and writing instruction—specifically, the place of literary realism and moral sensitivity as the ultimate goal of instruction. This preference reflects the literary taste of an educated elite, and, with its focus on nontechnological experience, it helps allay fears that children are missing out on "an authentic childhood" amidst the clutter of consumer goods and media seductions.

Many children who embrace that culture beg to differ.

There is, after all, no "view from nowhere," no place we can easily step into and escape the biases of race, gender, age, region, and, particularly, class. We are always *somewhere*. Maybe the best we can do is to recognize the fact that we are located and limited, and that our views of literacy are not inevitable, but connected to social-class tastes (and distastes), desires, and anxieties. In *The Unbearable Lightness of Being* (1984), Milan Kundera makes this mocking comment about the creation of self-interested hierarchies:

> The very beginning of Genesis tells us that God created man in order to give him dominion over fish and fowl and all creatures. Of course, Genesis was written by a man, not a horse. (286)

Those who construct the hierarchies inevitably put themselves at the apex. Some forms of literacy activity have status; other forms are barely recognized as literacy at all.

But, as we used to say on the playground, "Says who?"

# CHAPTER FIVE

# Violence and Innocence

Gardening consists largely in protecting plants from blight and weeds, and the same is true of attending to the growth of children. If a plant fails to grow properly because it is attacked by a pest, only a poor gardener would look for the cause in the plant alone. The good gardener will think immediately in terms of general precaution and spray the whole field. But with children we act like the bad gardener. We often fail to carry out elementary preventive measures.

—Fredric Wertham, 1953

**TN**: So you don't think that when you write about violence you might become violent?
**SARAH**: No, it's just a thing they say.

—Student interview

I n the wake of the Columbine shootings, many schools began to institute policies banning "violence" from school writing. As one school phrased it, kids were to keep violent themes and conflicts "at home." These restrictions prompted no outcry from the National Council of Teachers of English and other organizations that are typically so vigilant about issues of censorship. In fact, the restrictions may not have seemed like censorship at all, only the reasonable and civic response to these horrific shootings. The term *violence* is so emotionally loaded that it would appear irresponsible to try to make a case *for* it in any form. Yet that is what I will try to do in this chapter and the one that follows. In this one I will look broadly at claims about the effect of media violence on children; in the following chapter I will look more specifically at the function of violence in the writing of boys. But it is necessary to begin with a careful examination of the word *violence* itself.

A basic definition would go something like this: *Violence is the intentional infliction of pain (emotional or physical) on a living creature, obviously most serious when it is on another human being.* This definition might be extended to include the nonintentional infliction of pain (as in a violent car accident), but it is the combination of intent, action, and effect that is really the central concern. It might also include the destruction of property—but the human consequences are usually paramount. According to this definition, writing would be a violent act if it caused pain to others; if, for example, it caused readers to feel threatened or humiliated. For all the concern about physical violence, teasing is almost surely the most common form of violence in schools (see Lensmire 1994, 116–37).

"Fiction" that targets a teacher who not coincidentally resembles the student's actual teacher would be an example of violent writing. Similarly, a piece of fiction that humiliated another student could be called violent because of the effect it has. There are, of course, judgment calls involved—where does legitimate humor end and humiliation begin? What constitutes a legitimate threat? But I believe there is a distinction between writing that actually harms others and writing that represents harm coming to fictional characters. A *Roadrunner* cartoon is not "violent" in the sense I describe; i.e., it does not represent a threat (except maybe to coyotes), although it depicts, in a highly stylized and unrealistic way, a form of harm. Most of the student writing being banned in schools would seem to fall in this second category—writing that is not itself violent, but that depicts a form of violence.

I have found no evidence showing that students who employ violence in their stories actually commit violence (proving cause and effect would, in any case, be devilishly difficult). More likely, the case against writing that depicts violence rests on the claim made by many psychologists and pediatricians that media violence *does* promote violent behavior. A recent statement by the American Academy of Pediatricians (AAP) notes that by the age of eighteen, the average young person will have seen 200,000 acts of violence on television alone, often with three to five violent acts per hour. The report cites "conclusive" research evidence to show a causal connection between media violence and aggressive behavior. In fact, some researchers equate those who question this causal connection with those who deny the harmful effects of cigarettes. According to the report, the link is "undeniable and uncontestable" (Shevloe and Bar-on 1995, 2). One reason for this causal connection is the inability of younger children (and some immature older children, primarily boys) to distinguish between fantasy and reality—so the invariably violent conflict resolution in TV and movies becomes a model for behavior.

The AAP's statement then provides the third definition of violence: representations of harmful action that, while they pose no direct threat to teachers or classmates, still endorse inappropriate conflict resolution—and are therefore generally harmful. In this view, a *Star Wars*–like action adventure, with the forces of good killing off those of evil, is not innocent entertainment; it reinforces an unhealthy affection for weapons and combat in a world cleanly divided between Good and Bad.

## Censorship and Social Class;
## Anthony Comstock's Naked Lady Problem

Before looking at some of these rationales for excluding violence, I want to note one inconsistency in the argument. The violence of Great Literature is usually exempted from this prohibition (it's actually hard to imagine how literature could have been written under the rules imposed on students). No one seriously imagines that a reading of *Hamlet* will lead to fights with poisoned swords, or that a reading of *Oedipus Rex* will lead to poking out one's eyes or sleeping with one's mother. I have heard no concerns that reading "Hansel and Gretel" will lead children to imitate the witch and push their brothers or sisters into an oven.

If we look at the very first extended classic in English, *Beowulf*, we see almost exactly the kind of action writing that post-Columbine rules asked students to "keep at home." In the climactic scene Beowulf stabs Grendel so forcefully his sword snaps in two, leaving the blade in the bleeding monster, who thus enraged charges at Beowulf.

> The dangerous dragon, scourge of the Geats,
> was intent a third time upon attack; he rushed
> at the renowned man when he saw an opening:
> fiery, battle-grim, he gripped the hero's neck
> between his sharp teeth; Beowulf was bathed
> in blood; it spurted in streams. (1968, 106)

This is the stuff of child fantasies. It recalls a drawing given to me recently in which a five-year-old drew what he called the "Neck of Death," a two-headed dinosaur/monster who was simultaneously killing two humans, blood flying in a scribble of red. But in one case we are dealing with classic art—in the other, with the socially dangerous fantasies of young boys.

Why, then, is violent content in classical literature perceived as nonthreatening (even uplifting and humanizing), when the same violent content in more popular media is seen as provocative and dangerous? The answer may reside not in the representation of violence, but in the way the *audience* for that violence is imagined. The reader of classic literature, or someone who rented the incredibly violent movie *Titus* (a rendition of Shakespeare's *Titus Andronicus*) would be assumed to be part of a nonviolent literate social class who would approach the book or film with the proper aesthetic distance. There would be no danger of suggestibility in these activities because they would be intelligently mediated by the reader or viewer. No such assumption is made about someone watching a much less graphically violent movie, such as one from the *Lethal Weapon* series. The nonelite group that chooses to watch the more popular versions of violence is perceived as more susceptible to suggestion, less capable of keeping the proper distance, more volatile. All of which leads to the question, Is the issue really about violence, or is it about the social class (and age group) the violence appeals to?

This issue of social-class differential was central to one of the great censorship waves in this country. After the Civil War, Anthony Comstock began his crusade against "immorality." Among his targets was "pornographic" artwork depicting female nudity (another was all forms of birth control—even dispensing information on the topic). He especially targeted the postcard-type reproductions that could be easily purchased for less than a dollar. But condemning all nude art put him in conflict with the art dealers who sold to a wealthy and powerful clientele whose support Comstock needed. Consequently, he needed to establish a rationale for banning cheap reproductions of art while acknowledging the artistic function of the paintings in the homes of the aristocracy. Accordingly, Comstock claimed that the "artistic" qualities were totally lost in smaller reproductions:

> A grand oil painting, with its massive coloring, its artistic surroundings, its grand shadings, and streaks of light, all of which

create a work of art, ceases to be such when represented in a photograph, which gives the mere outline of the form, and that is all.
(Quoted in Beisel 1997, 177)

But the real issue for Comstock was not the qualities of the art, but
who had access to it. Only a certain social class could enter the
"surroundings" where original works of art were exhibited, and
this class could be trusted to view nudity with a proper nonerotic
perspective. The "masses" could not be similarly trusted:

> . . . Let me add, if you please, that the very cost of art precludes it
> from being gaped at—stared at by the masses, who have no con-
> ception of the grandeur of the merits of such a work—and would,
> if they had the chance, merely admire the very form, the bare nudity
> if you so call it, without letting their minds or their eyes, even if they
> could, rest upon the grand surroundings; in fact, upon the work of
> art as an entirety. (177)

This wealthy clientele had the restraint not to look at nudity itself
and diverted their gaze to the "surroundings." It's as if they fixated
on the ornate frames. Comstock's solution was to seize cheap
reproductions, but to allow any copies costing more than ten dol-
lars to be distributed. This restriction would put them out of range
of an impressionable immigrant population.

Thus the inevitable logic of censorship—to claim that some
art has a negative impact on *others*, while exempting the censor-
ing class from those proclivities.

## Gandhi and the Punch Toy

The AAP report claims that the debate about the effects of media
on children is over. Yet it clearly is not. It would be a monumental
digression to review the mass of data that presumably supports
this claim, but I do want to note the criticisms that have come from
a group of revisionist researchers who have challenged the naive

behaviorism—the "effects paradigm"—that underlies this body of work. Typically these studies consist of a stimulus, such as watching a violent movie, followed by the monitoring of the "effect," sometimes the changed attitudes of the subjects or their immediate behavior (e.g., the number of aggressive acts on the playground). Joseph Tobin caustically describes this methodology:

> The researchers typically show children violent movies in a laboratory setting and then monitor their reactions, usually by leaving them alone with a Bobo (punching bag) doll and watching through a one-way mirror to see what happens. Critics point out that these experiments "measure artificial responses to artificial stimuli in artificial situations" (Buckingham 1993, 11). What would you expect a child to do with a punch doll other than punch it? Under these conditions even Gandhi might have been tempted to throw a few jabs. (2000, 16–17)

The approach is circular, assuming what it presumes to prove. It is assumed that the children have nothing interesting to say about the visual stimulus—so they aren't asked. The film is treated not as a text that is interpreted by the child, not as something processed in any way. The child is presumed to have virtually no capacity to interpret, to resist or to mediate.

When TV or film is called a "drug" the same assumption is made—the medium acts in a direct way upon the child who, after all, cannot decide to resist the effect of a carcinogen. There may be differing thresholds of effect; not all smokers develop lung cancer, just as not all TV watchers are provoked to violence. But there is no interpretation, no resistance, no real mental activity on the part of the viewers, particularly if they are young. As one media critic categorically states, "Watching television not only requires no skills but develops no skills" (Postman 1982, 79). Typically, this research emphasizes the vulnerability of *others*. David Buckingham writes:

> Effects, it would seem, are things from which others suffer. We ourselves . . . are somehow immune . . . These other people are seen

as being unable to distinguish between fiction and reality. They are somehow too immature or mentally inadequate to know any better. (1996, 65)

In this huge body of work, students were rarely interviewed or allowed to discuss reactions or interpretations—because it was assumed they did not have real interpretations, only responses to stimuli.

One of the common cautions about TV violence, one repeated in the AAP statement, is that young children cannot reliably distinguish between reality and fantasy. Paradoxically, this was a concern about *books* and silent independent reading in the Renaissance—one popular comic figure was the "book fool," bespectacled and cut off from the world (Manguel 1996, 291–303). The fear was that independent reading in isolation might foster a form of madness where fantasy and reality were entangled, and the first great novel of the period, *Don Quixote*, of course, plays with this possibility.

In fact, it was the researchers in many of these studies who had this difficulty, failing to distinguish between the "aggression" of fantasy play and aggression with the intention to harm. Take for example a relatively recent study that attempted to measure the effect on elementary school children immediately after viewing an episode of *Mighty Morphin Power Rangers* in their school (Boyatzis and Matillo 1995). The researchers coded the "aggressive" behavior of both the experimental group, which watched the video, and a control group that didn't. Aggressive actions might include verbal action (speaking or yelling in an insulting way) and physical action (hitting, pushing, tripping, throwing objects at each other). Not surprisingly, the study finds that the experimental group (particularly the boys in that group) "committed more aggressive acts" than the control group, a discovery the researchers find both "important and alarming" (5).

Unlike some earlier "effects" studies, this one tries to link TV watching with actual behavior and not the kind of contrived measure Buckingham criticized. So one might see it as a state-of-the-art example of how effects research is carried out. Yet the central problem in the design is the failure to distinguish between behavior that is truly violent (i.e., intentionally inflicting harm) and imitative play that one could easily imagine occurring among friends. Undoubtedly this "aggressive" action took the form of children reenacting some of the martial moves, the karate chops and kicks, accompanied by sound effects. Simply coding the *behavior* prevents the researchers from reading the intention of the actions, and this failure to read intention also allows them to stigmatize the imitative play following the video as "aggression," a category loaded with social disapproval. By not distinguishing between active play and real-life aggression, the researchers, it seems to me, fail the very test they accuse children of failing—distinguishing between fantasy and reality. Even if such studies were replicated indefinitely, they would fail to make the case.

Undoubtedly there are developmental issues in developing a sure sense of the distinction between fantasy and real-world causality and limitations. And there *are* alarming cases of imitative violence. But even with young children, this difficulty is regularly overstated. Malcolm Gladwell tells an instructive story about the development of *Sesame Street* in his book *The Tipping Point* (2000). While *Sesame Street* came to be one of the most popular and beloved children's TV shows, it had serious problems well into the developmental stages. Children didn't like it. Originally the developers followed the advice of developmental psychologists, who warned about mixing the "real" characters and the "fantasy" characters (e.g., having Big Bird talk to Maria). This mixing of real and unreal, the psychologists warned, would be confusing to children for whom the distinction is shaky. Finally, in desperation, the developers decided to reject this advice, to mix the fantasy and human characters. The rest, as they say, is history. Children had no problem with the mixture.

Those who make the case for imitative violence have to deal with the example of Japan, where children's programming is typically more violent than it is in the United States. The *Mighty Morphin Power Rangers*, a big hit in the early 1990s, was a Japanese import, as are many of the action cartoons currently on the Warner Brothers and Fox networks. The newer imported cartoons, called *anime*, feature almost nonstop fighting—buildings explode, heroes are attacked by razors, bodies disintegrate (Rutenberg 2001). According the logic of the "effects" research, if this is the standard fare for Japanese children, one would expect that there would be a major problem of violence in Japanese society—yet the crime rate is one of the world's lowest, most likely due to stable social structures and lack of access to guns.

Another problem with research summaries like that contained in the AAP statement is the incompatible mix of claims. We are told that TV watching leads to imitative action—and to desensitization; that is, it acts both as a stimulant and a depressant. The claim for desensitization rests on the seemingly commonsensical observation that the exposure to any repeated action leads to the dulling of sensibility. If kids by the age of eighteen have seen 200,000 simulated killings on TV, how could they *not* be desensitized?

The logic holds only if we accept that the simulated, often highly stylized, depictions of violence on TV work the same way as actual, experienced violence. Normally we would assume that to be "desensitized" to *X* (say, cigarette smoke), we would need to be regularly in the presence of *X*. Watching others in the presence of *X* won't do it. Soldiers in combat can become desensitized to the death around them (they may need to in order to maintain sanity); Don Murray, a veteran of the Battle of the Bulge, tells of how during a break to eat he found himself sitting on the body of a dead priest, something he found *funny* at the time (2001). That's desensitization.

The argument for TV's desensitization rests on the reality vs. fantasy claim. IF children cannot distinguish fantasy from reality, then desensitization can occur because the simulations of violence can have the effect of real violence (after all, the child can't distinguish them). The *Challenger* explosion of 1986 put this claim to an interesting test: if regular exposure to types of simulated violence are "desensitizing," then surely children would be desensitized to explosions in space. The exploding spaceship is a staple of action movies, and it has been drawn and redrawn by generations of boys. Yet when an explosion was *real*, killing a real teacher, some- one like the teacher standing before them, the event was a fright- ening reminder that life can be lost in an instant. It was a qualitatively different experience.

Similarly, student reaction to the Columbine shootings does not suggest a population desensitized to violence; for many it was the defining emotional moment of their lives (as least until it was overtaken by the World Trade Center disaster), as evidenced by the number who wrote about it on college admission essays. As one admissions director put it, the Columbine shootings "seems to have called young people out of themselves more than any event we have seen. It has taken them to a new level of awareness. They are asking, 'Who am I? What is my community like?'" (Langland 2001). Although school violence has been a staple in movies like *Carrie* and the cult favorite *Heathers*, it is different and threatening when it is real. The ultimate act of terror in our lives, the attack on the World Trade Center, was anticipated in movies like *The Tow- ering Inferno* and *Black Sunday*, but none of these could emotion- ally prepare us for—or desensitize us to—the reality we saw, again and again, on our televisions. We experienced the real attack as a qualitatively different experience.

One final problem with traditional research on media violence needs to be noted. Few shows that contain violence are about *only* violence; most action movies also stress teamwork, loyalty, perse- verance, ingenuity, problem solving, stoicism, athletic fitness, courage, and frequently patriotism. The action hero typically has to overcome adversity, failure, and sometimes discouragement at having to face a superior force. If 200,000 exposures to violence cause a person to be violent, does the same number of exposures to teamwork create an ethic of cooperation? Does 200,000 expo- sures to ingenuity create a desire to be ingenious? Why should one message—that of the acceptability of violence—be the sole effect of these shows when even cartoons are about much more than that? The alarmist claims about the effects of media violence rest on research that reduces complex narratives with multiple messages to simple "stimuli" that work automatically, like a carcino-gen, at an unconscious level. Not only is the media narrative reduced; the young viewers too are reduced, to being unconscious reactors with no interpretive resources.

## Kids Make the Case for Violence

When we interview kids about violence and their right to use it, something new is introduced to the debate—*nuance*. They make distinctions about gradations of violence, types of violence, degrees of receptivity to violence. They explain what they see as the necessity of violence in some genres of writing that rely on sus-pense. What struck me most about the kids I interviewed was their willingness to accept *limits*, including their own; that is, they didn't take a libertarian position that there should be no restrictions on what they write and see. A media environment *without restrictions* would be frightening to them. Although they frequently bragged about seeing movies they were legally restricted from, they recog-nized the need for restrictions, coding, and limits. So their desire for action and conflict, even for excess and escape, *exists within a system of comprehensible rules.*

A few years ago, during a difficult period in high school, my nephew spent much of his spare time playing the violent shooter game Rise of the Triad. At the beginning of each game he could set the level of violence he wanted, and he always chose the cat-egory "excessive." It seemed paradoxical that "excessive" could be a category, since excess is by definition uncontained. As I watched him play, dazzled by his ability to anticipate the enemy and shift tactics, it occurred to me that the mayhem of this game was actu-ally a tightly controlled environment that he had mastered. How-ever powerless he might have felt in school, once he logged on to Rise of the Triad, he was in charge.

In her wonderful book on violent children's play, *Under Dead-man's Skin* (2001), Jane Katch describes this curious mix of imagi-native excess operating within negotiated legalistic school rules.

She had tried since the beginning of the school year to enforce three rules for recess play: no excessive blood, no chopping off of body parts, and no guts or other things that belong in the body falling out. Several of the students complained that these rules were too restrictive and that they didn't see why kids who weren't bothered by this kind of play shouldn't do it. One child began to loudly spell out "V-O-A-T" (he'd just learned the vowel rule), and the class voted to allow violent play on alternate recesses. Violent play would be permitted—but scheduled.

Films, even violent ones, often operate within limitations which keep them from threatening viewers. The film critic David Denby has described the "comfort" American viewers paradoxically get from cinematic violence:

> In the American cinema, violence breathes comfortably within the confines of genre movies: action films, crime pictures, thrillers. The conventions of such movies both release the formal beauty of violence and remove it from a world that might threaten us. When violence is aestheticized, converted into style, we can enjoy it— even enjoy it ten or fifteen times a year. But violence unpropped by convention—that is, violence converted into pain—is something of a rarity. (1999b)

The violence is made "safe" in a number of ways: by removing it from human pain, by withholding some of its graphic consequences, by interspersing it with humor (the jokiness of James Bond movies reminds us not to take things seriously), and by using it in the service of a good cause like saving the planet. We can also be drawn to the stylized beauty of action. In the movie *Matrix*, there is a violent gun scene in which dozens of security guards are killed, but we are drawn to the sleek, sexy gracefulness of the two protagonists, dressed in black leather, and to the slow-motion images of empty shell casings bouncing off the floor.

For the boys I interviewed, "blood" was the signifier of violence, and they were often amazingly articulate about how bleeding should be handled. Andrew, a fourth grader, takes his cue from the graveyard scene in *The Adventures of Tom Sawyer*, which had been read to the class:

**ANDREW:** Like if you're going to write horror, is horror too violent? It might have a teeny bit but not too violent like stabbing people and blood dripping everywhere.

**TN:** Do you think it's okay to have some blood in a story?

**ANDREW:** Yeah, not too much because the reader won't get interested if there is too much blood in it.

He then cites as a model the way Twain describes the bleeding in the violent graveyard scene. Curious, I looked up that scene. Here is how Twain describes the bleeding of Dr. Williams, who is stabbed by Injun Joe:

> He reeled and fell partly on Potter [who was helping Williams excavate a corpse], flooding him with blood, and in the same moment the clouds blotted out the dreadful spectacle and the two frightened boys went speeding away in the dark. ([1876] 1974, 95)

Less than one full sentence on the effects of the stabbing, with the clouds opportunely blocking the moon and sparing the boys any more detail. It's violent enough.

We can see an even more elaborate discussion of these limits in this exchange between two fifth graders:

**CASEY:** A little bit's pretty cool. If it's perfect it's really, really cool. If there's too much it's like ooooh.

**TN:** So it has to be just right or . . .

**CASEY:** Perfect or a little bit less, because if it's too much it's ahhhhh.

**TN:** Can you think of a movie that has too much?

**CASEY:** Let me think. *Terminator*—way too much blood.

**MORGAN:** I saw *Child's Play 2*.

**CASEY:** All of them have blood, too much. But *The Mask of Zorro*, I've seen that movie, and it has just the right amount of blood coming from disconnecting his neck from his body. It makes you think, "cool."

MORGAN: I like how they do that. They take the dummies and like fill them with red paint.

CASEY: You know it's not real, but it looks real.

MORGAN: And they cut. A few minutes before they cut, they stop and bring the dummy in and they'll cut the dummy's head off, and the red paint comes out.

CASEY: Cool, cool. Just the right amount. And you know it's fake, and you think it's cool.

MORGAN: It sends chills up your back, too.

CASEY: Like, that's got to hurt.

TN: So do you have just the right amount of blood in your story?

CASEY: There's not a lot of blood there; there's only droplets of blood that come before they disintegrate.

What's striking about this conversation is the double perspective the students maintain. On one hand, they can react to the violence as if it were real ("That's got to hurt"; "It sends chills up your back"). On the other hand, there is the comforting or protecting sense of artifice—"You know it's fake, and you think it's cool." Casey also argued for another form of protection, the "right" amount of blood; we don't get the pulsing spurts from a truly severed jugular vein.

I suspect that Morgan, who volunteers that he has seen the R-rated *Child's Play 2,* may be more eager to move outside the safety zone that Casey describes. Just as Vygotsky describes a "zone of proximal development" (1978), a set of manageable challenges for the learner, kids like Morgan may seek out manageable challenges to their own fearfulness. They test their own nerve by watching movies like *Child's Play 2* to see if they can handle the terror. His claim to have watched the movie is a double boast: I'm not bound by rules that will keep me from it—and I can take it.

As Tobin notes, some of this boasting can be read as self-parody as the boys perform the part of bloodthirsty male action-film addicts. We catch something of that performativity in this exchange following a question about the difference between boys' and girls' writing:

EVAN: Like girls write about animals and stuff like that, while boys write about wars and violence—like having bears tear faces off. (*Laughs*) They don't tear anybody's face off, but . . .

JIM: And we like write stories about planes that blow up and stuff like piranhas. Like in Sean's story he hits it with an oar and says, "Die beastie." (*Laughs*)

Boys often claim a sense of superiority over girls because of their capacity to "take" violence and gore. As one stated categorically, "Girls are more afraid." But when he began to describe the goriness of his own stories, he responded like Jake above, citing an example that was undercut by humor and parody, that approached the cartoon level of reality (in his case it was an anaconda squeezing a panther until his eyes popped out). It was safely unrealistic violence, operating within clear limits on explicitness.

Blood is the great signifier in these discussions, the gauge of violence, and the kids I interviewed would, like Casey, base their limits on the acceptable amount of blood. In the following discussion I asked two fourth graders to spell out these limits with references to two multisequel movies that all three of us knew, the *Star Wars* trilogy and the *Indiana Jones* series. Mark begins by making a distinction between suspense and violence:

MARK: It's not that exciting explaining how the blood is, like what's happening. I think it's more exciting when you have less violence. I think it's more exciting like if someone's in a book and they saw something but they didn't know what it is. I think it's more scary and more exciting. If you can find out what it is it's less exciting, because you know what it is. But if you only saw something for a second you don't know what it is. I think it's more exciting and scarier.

Thus a hint of danger or threat is more effective, scarier, than overt violence. I ask about *Star Wars*:

**ANDREW:** You don't have blood everywhere. You just have people die. That show, I think is a good show. It doesn't have too much violence because they have bad guys and the good guys are trying to save the galaxy. So I think that's a good show because there's not blood running everywhere and like they kill people to save the galaxy, and the imperial dudes kill the rebels to conquer the galaxy, to rule another country where people own land. Nobody owns the galaxy.

This might be seen as a political justification, a version of Augustine's "just war" theory: measured violence can be justified to resist the imperial invasion of the Death Star.

Mark picks up on the issue of blood, reminding me of something I'd forgotten, that most of those "killed" in the *Star Wars* movies are machines:

**MARK:** Well in *Star Wars*, it's not like gunshots and monsters that pick you up and blood flies everywhere. If anyone gets killed in that, it's just like a black hole, and humans usually don't get killed because some of them are machines and it's usually not that bloody—and it can be exciting.

I switched to the *Indiana Jones* movies, where the violence is more realistic. I asked if they were "too violent":

**MARK:** It can be if you are very young because sometimes there are dangerous spots. People, like, get killed. They were in this temple and someone gets a spear through them. It was violent but it can be exciting too.
**ANDREW:** I think some parts of it aren't too violent but some parts are. I've seen one episode where Indiana Jones was with the Indians and the Indians were shooting bows and arrows at the bad dudes, the bad guys, and when they die they fall down

this huge cliff into the water and get eaten by alligators and blood was everywhere, their shirts were falling off and floating in the water. So you could see their shirts but not their skin anywhere. But you could see blood in the water.

**TN:** It sounds like you like that part.

**ANDREW:** Not really.

**TN:** Not really?

**ANDREW:** I like the part where they fall down and the part where they get eaten by alligators, but not the blood part or when you see the shirts but not them.

Andrew is making a distinction between action and the graphic depictions of the results of the action (the blood). Mark picks up this point, making a distinction between what he calls "excitement" and "violence."

**MARK:** In Indiana Jones, the exciting parts, they sort of happen at the mix, *while it is happening,* when they're still in combat with another person and they're half and half, none of them could get to each other. Then it's exciting because which of them is going to win and when someone wins, it's not that exciting because there's blood everywhere.

**ANDREW:** You may think it's violent for rats and mice to come up and be eating the guy or when he's dead and the person's still stabbing him when he's dead and kicking him around. I think that's violent.

In almost every conversation, I was the one introducing the morally loaded term "violence"; the kids I interviewed invariably used "action" or "excitement," or even "suspense." Their major concern was with the onward movement of story, and they did not dwell on details about the consequences, the physical harm, of the "action."

Media critics might warn that this disconnection, this consequence-less violence, develops the false notion that physical aggression has no harmful effects (again invoking the breakdown of the fantasy/reality barrier). But one suspects that if children *did* dwell graphically on these effects, the "desensitization" argument would be invoked. It would be argued that repeated detailed renderings of human pain and injury would dull their moral sensitivity: Kids would get used to suffering. In other words, they're cornered.

While the kids I interviewed accepted, even endorsed, limits on the depiction of violence, they adamantly insisted on the necessity of violence in their stories, particularly their favorite genre of fiction, horror stories (Millard 2001). Their position is consistent with that of media researchers Robert Hodge and David Tripp, who claim that violence "is a natural signifier of conflict and difference, and without representations of conflict, art of the past and present would be seriously impoverished" (1986, 217). Typically, I would ask students how they would react, or argue against a hypothetical (or not so hypothetical) rule that would prohibit all violence in student writing. Here is the exchange with a pair of fourth graders:

ETHAN: You need violence to have an adventure. And you need some death to have an adventure story—for the main character to go out and have a reason to go out, like a big journey or something.

Ethan also enjoyed writing detective stories where, as he claims, violence is the trigger for the plot. I asked his partner, Rachael, the same question:

RACHAEL: Well in one of our assignments we had to write a scary story and when you write it you have to have violence in it most of the time because it's not that scary if you just said, "A monster came." That would work sometimes with little kids, but it wouldn't scare me that much. But, like, violence would make me more scared, and you, like, sort of need more violence.

The stories they were attempting to write relied on suspense, on fear and feeling threatened—effects that require some form of violence. To categorically prohibit violence would make such writing impossible.

When I asked about the possible negative effects this violence might have on them, I was often met with blank looks. They could understand limitations that kept them from violent material that might scare them too much or give them nightmares. But once they understood my question about the relation of violent material *to their own behavior*, most simply dismissed the possibility. I realize that effects researchers would claim that the children couldn't gauge this effect for themselves; still, in fairness, their denials should be heard:

RACHAEL: Like, my family is pretty religious and violence wouldn't help and violence wouldn't make anyone like you. It could get you into habits that could kill you. But if you read or write violence, that shouldn't affect you so much because it's fake. Most of the stuff that's violence is fake, and so if it's fake you shouldn't act like fake stuff.

The boundary line between the violent fantasies of writing—and actual violent behavior—was, in Rachael's mind, absolutely clear.

Probably the most poignant denial came from a third grader struggling to find words to describe how his own moral code would keep him from violent acts. I asked him if it would be a good rule to ban all violence and shooting in kids' stories (which was actually a loosely enforced rule in the school):

ALEX: Not really.
TN: Why "not really?"
ALEX: Well, that's what we have.
TN: What do you mean "what we have?"
ALEX: It's part of the action, guns and stuff.
TN: Suppose I say that if we let you write that stuff it will make you more likely to hit or hurt people. Do you think that's true?
ALEX: No.

**TN:** Why not?

**ALEX:** Because I put stuff in my head. I really want to get good grades, and I really think about things, and I make sure I don't do what I'm not supposed to do.

**TN:** So when you read about someone who shoots someone, that wouldn't change what you would do?

**ALEX:** Well, yes. I know that people want to live and they don't want to die and if there's shooting they're going to die. Now if it was a war, I'd have to fight—but I'd try to miss.

Students categorically dismissed the question as it concerned them and their classmates, but they did not entirely reject the possibility for more susceptible kids. They could imagine a type who might be affected, confirming Tobin's claim that the negative effects of media are typically thought to affect *someone else*. Ethan uses the term "intense" to describe the type who might be vulnerable:

**ETHAN:** I don't think it would affect me. But some people that are into that love movies with killing and shooting. Every story they write there's a gun in it; I think that *would* affect them in their life. I mean practically everyone in our class—that wouldn't affect them because I don't think anybody in our class is intense on killing people, you know like stories with death in it. So I think it would affect some people—but not, like, kids. Maybe, like, older people that see this movie that they really want to see and it seems so real to them that they really want to try something. Like, people that are really intense would do that.

Interestingly, Ethan sees "older people" as more likely to be moved to imitative violence.

Jane Katch reports an almost identical discussion with a ten-year-old boy who is sorting out his opinions about the violent video games he loves to play. In the interview Jason states that, "Violent videos help people take it [their frustration and unhappiness] the wrong way, encourage them to be violent." Katch asks if he thinks that about himself, and Jason provides this complex answer:

> It's sort of weird. Because I think they're bad and I don't think they should be played by kids my age, but if I couldn't play them I'd be pretty mad, you know so it's sort of weird. I like and enjoy them but I don't think I should like and enjoy them. I don't agree with myself on them, you know?
>
> I used to think that they helped you take out violence. I don't think they really encourage violence for me. I don't have really enough aggression to make it necessary for me to have them, so like, they don't really do a good thing for me. But I don't think they do anything bad for me, either. (2001, 119)

His statement is powerfully contradictory. The games promote violence, but not for him. Because he experiences moderate aggression, the games are not "necessary for him"—though, by implication, they might be for someone with more powerful aggressive feelings (yet are these the very people who might be in more need of an outlet?). Violent video games are "bad," yet he enjoys them (does that make *him* bad?).

Katch wisely interprets Jason's ambivalence to be more about his own anxiety about the intensity of his own aggression than about the games themselves. She provides the best explanation I have seen for the psychological function these games serve:

> For a kid who often feels powerless in relation to adults and other kids, the video games are a safe way he can feel strong and in control. After a bad day at school he can go to his room and peacefully kill off the enemies, making steady progress toward an attainable goal. With a video game anyone can be a dominant puppy. It's a satisfaction in his life that he can count on. Why should he give it up? (120)

The video games provide a release, a way of containing and chan-
neling aggression.

The central drama of Katch's wonderful book *Under Deadman's
Skin* is her own personal attempt to understand the place of violence in children's play. She describes the repugnance she feels
toward much of this play, and despite this repugnance her attempt
to listen to children to see the function it serves. Throughout the
book she recalls the training she received from Bruno Bettelheim,
and particularly a key passage from *The Uses of Enchantment* (1989):

> Parents who wish to deny that their child has murderous wishes and
> wants to tear things and even people into pieces believe that their
> child must be prevented from engaging in such thoughts (as if this
> were possible). By denying access to stories which implicitly tell the
> child that others have the same fantasies, he is left to feel that he is
> the only one who imagines such things. This makes his fantasies
> really scary. On the other hand, learning that others have the same
> or similar fantasies makes us feel that we are part of humanity, and
> allays our fears that having destructive ideas has put us beyond the
> common pale. (122)

Aggression, for Bettelheim, is not some "external" idea planted in
children's pliant heads by the media; it is part of our shared nature
as human beings.

While most of the students I interviewed treated violence in
writing as a form of imaginative play, a few described precisely the
sublimating function Bettelheim names. Here is an exchange
between Sarah and her partner, Bradley:

SARAH: You think about it [anger and violence] so much, and
    nobody will let you get it out. Like your friends. You try to talk
    to them about it, and so you get very upset about the subject
    and everything, and they just might not let you get it out, and
    so one day you'll become that bad guy too.

BRADLEY: Well they [kids' stories] have a lot of violence, but, like
    Sarah said, they have to get it out of their system, because if

they don't do it in their writing, and they can't do it in real life, what happens to it? It builds up into anger and hate.

This view is consistent with an Aristotelian description of art as a form of purification or purging of emotions like pity and fear (see also Feshbach 1961), a position that has undercut the behaviorist depiction of media violence as a pure stimulus to more violence.

I offer these sections from interviews not to show in any definitive way what children think. That would take a far bigger project. I cannot even claim to have gone to the bedrock of what these children actually think; as Erving Goffman (1959) reminds us, all social situations call for a performance of self, a reading of the situation and the taking on of a role. The children were performing for me (as I performed the "researcher" for them). The self revealed in interviews is, undoubtedly, not identical to the self that sneaks in, underage, to *Anaconda* and delights when a victim is squeezed so hard his eyeballs pop out.

But I *do* claim that talking with children takes us beyond the crude monolithic concept of "violence," that unfortunate legacy of the "effects" research paradigm. Paradoxically, they introduce complexity to the topic; they make distinctions; they argue for and against limits; they examine the place of types of violence in various genres. They remind us of what we miss when violence is banned, rather than discussed.

## Childhood, Violence, and Adult Desire

The belief that children need protection from displays of violence comes from a belief in their inability to protect themselves, in a fragility that has not always been associated with childhood. The French historian Philippe Aries claims that childhood itself is a relatively recent cultural invention. Up until the seventeenth century, children worked alongside adults and dressed like adults. According to Aries, they were exposed to sexual jokes (sometimes at their own expense) and, if the paintings of Pieter Brueghel the

Elder are any indication, they were not protected from adult displays of drunkenness, fighting, and sexual activity. Parents weren't concerned about them being corrupted, because the very concept of childhood as a separate "innocent" stage of life is a later cultural construction. Around the beginning of the seventeenth century, a new pedagogical and devotional literature began to appear that stressed the angelic purity of childhood, a divine incapacity that needed the protection and guidance of schools. Pamphlets warned that children should not be left alone, that they should not be allowed to learn modern songs or attend puppet shows, or to sleep in the same bed with other children. Childhood was exalted as an Edenic stage of life—and it was tightly reined in. We have inherited this conception, this invention of childhood, with all its tensions.

Cultural historians, building on Aries' work, stress that the myth of childhood innocence "empties the child of its own political agency, so that it may more perfectly fulfill the symbolic needs we make upon it" (Jenkins 1998, 1). As James Kincaid describes, the child (and by extension the school that educates the child) becomes a repository for cultural anxiety and fears:

> The child was there waiting . . . defenseless and alluring, with no substance, no threatening history, no independent insistencies. As a category created but not occupied, the child could be a repository of cultural needs or fears not adequately disposed of elsewhere. . . . The child carries for us things we cannot carry for ourselves, sometimes anxieties we want to be divorced from and sometimes pleasures so great we would not, without the child, know how to contain them. (Quoted in Jenkins 1998, 4)

The metaphors used in the condemnation and prohibition of media violence invariably invoke some version of this Myth of Innocence. Almost any argument for censorship relies on it. Fredric Wertham titled his book *Seduction of the Innocent*, turning comic books, and their creators, into sleazy sexual predators enticing the defenseless. Media violence is also a drug, a poison, an electric charge, a cancer, a form of pollution—all of which attack a body unable to defend itself. Always the harm is coming from "outside" sources. But how does this construction, this negative combative imagery, help us deal with "cultural needs or fears not adequately disposed of elsewhere?" Where's the comfort in it?

Undoubtedly most parents get some comfort from imagining childhood as a space free of deep anxieties, doubts, and failures. And perhaps these metaphors affirm a parental sense that children are possessions—they are *ours*, to protect and nurture in the safe place of home. Risk comes not from within the home (despite all evidence to the contrary), but from malign forces that come from "outside" and infiltrate the home via coaxial cable. "Hollywood," MTV, the creators of video games are the real pushers, the predators who lurk on street corners trying to hook our kids. Literacy, books, and schooling are imagined as antidotes, vaccines, forms of resistance to the addicting power of visual media. The goal, to borrow Daniel Fader's famous title from the late 1960s, is to be *Hooked on Books*, or more currently to be *Hooked on Phonics*. Literacy in almost any form is a morally good thing; it's the right kind of addiction (though not for Don Quixote).

I am, of course, arguing something different. According to Aries, the modern conception of childhood puts a burden of surveillance upon parents and schools. As Anthony Comstock put it in his characteristically flamboyant way:

> Let fathers, mothers, and teachers watch closely over the pockets, desks, and rooms of their children. Be sure that the seeds of moral death are not in your homes and schools. (Beisel 1997, 71)

Of course parenting *does* involve watchfulness, although usually not to the paranoid degree Comstock urges. But the effect of *being watched* creates for kids a desire for places and fictions where they have power. As one third grader put it, "In fiction you make your own personal world, your own world, your own rules." Anne Dyson argues that "at the heart of child culture is the desire for a space in which children, not adults, have control" (1999, 394).

Many of the low-status fictions, the unrealistic and "violent" ones, speak to this desire for power.

We can see this desire for free space in the phenomenal attraction of professional wrestling. It is almost part of the script for adults to disapprove of the "violence" of professional wrestling. But look what happens to the referee—conventionally the "adult" in the ring, the father figure, the one who sees that things go according to the rules. In official sports, the referee opens an event with fatherly warnings and encouragement to the athletes, performing as the good, wise, but strict parent that we're all supposed to crave.

But in professional wrestling, the referees are feckless. The match usually starts without this ceremony, usually initiated by the combatants. And at key moments in the match, the referee gets in the way of a lunge or leap or punch, and with him then senseless on the mat, the fight continues—in a free, unsupervised space.

# CHAPTER SIX

# Misreading Violence

"I love missions—blowing the scrap out of people."
—A fourth grader

T he research on boys' writing is much less extensive than the more general—and politically loaded—investigations of media violence. Yet in most of it there is the same misreading, the same literalism, the same moralistic tone of disapproval. To label writing as "violent" automatically invokes a set of social attitudes and fears, particularly anxiety about the propensity of boys to ultimately act out their "violent" fantasies. It is such a potent term that researchers typically can move from their findings about "violent" themes in boys' writing (however loosely defined) to a sense of alarm, followed by proposals to channel this writing in more socially constructive directions.

I will briefly summarize one recent study to analyze the state of the art in writing research that relies on content analysis of writing themes. Mary Ann and Thomas Gray-Schlegel (1995–1996) asked a group of third and sixth graders to complete stories that came from two "story starters":

His/her first thought as s/he woke up was, "Today is the day."
AND
S/he looked around to see what made the noise.

One of the themes the researchers looked for was the inclusion of violence in the stories, and not surprisingly they found that 61 percent of the boys' stories contained some reference to violence or crime (neither term being defined). While the incidence was higher than in girls' writing, by sixth grade girls included these elements in 40 percent of the stories (compared to only 5 percent in third grade). The researchers call this result "disturbing" and encourage teachers to be "change agents" modeling more socially appropriate narratives, including those in which male characters are seen in nurturing roles.

Joseph Tobin might claim that the second prompt—asking students to imagine an unexpected noise—is the verbal equivalent of the punch toy. It invites the introduction of violence. The "noise" can be taken to signify some threat, some intrusion, even a crime, which can lead to the need for detection. The greater use of "violence" among the older students might show their greater facility in using these openings to direct them to the genres they typically like to read (and watch), to plots of adventure, detection, and horror, all of which involve physical threat. While the call for expanding the range of possibilities for children is well taken, this study is typical in failing to explore the psychological gratification children gain from producing this writing (or the skill involved in producing the stories). By labeling the writing "violent" and "stereotypical," the authors of the study dismiss it by invoking morally charged labels.

This research shows that in addition to including more violence in their stories, the boys create major protagonists who often act alone where girls tends to focus on joint action, on working with others in community (McAuliffe 1993–1994; Trepanier-Street, Romatowski, and McNair 1990). As I wrote in Chapter 1, Carol Gilligan (1982) noted similar differences in her story-completion tasks and concluded that this isolation shows a deeply ingrained male fear of intimacy and affiliation. Yet conclusions like this fail to account for the often-collaborative ways in which these "isolated" heroes are created, the active give-and-take of the boys' writing table (Dyson 1993). There is often a deeply *social* subtext to stories that might appear individualistic and combative. For many or even most boys it makes no sense to claim that competition (or conflict) and collaboration are *opposed* ideals; rather, boys regularly collaborate *through* combative play.

## Violence as a Mode of Friendship

A literal reading of boys' writing can easily lead to the bleak conclusion that they create worlds of conflict, danger, and isolation in which there are only fleeting pleasures that come not from friendship but from momentary dominance. By contrast, young girls regularly and openly describe their friendships, as Mandy, a fourth grader, does in her tribute to Lindsay, which begins:

> "Go Lindsay" I yell as Lindsay my best friend dives into the water. Lindsay and I always do swim team together. I walk down the side of the pool to congratulate Lindsay. Lindsay is a very special person in my life. We do all different kinds of wonderful stuff together. We both have special memories of our special times together that we will always keep in our hearts.

This style of direct affirmation is simply not available to most boys. As William Pollack claims, there is a code of boyhood that would prohibit such directness. A boy writing in this way would be extraordinarily vulnerable. His very status as a male might possibly called into question by being so directly affectionate to a member of his own sex.

Yet just because this code is denied them, that does not mean that boys lack a code for expressing friendship and affection. It *does* mean that affirmations of friendship must be converted to less direct, more oblique forms. Sometimes I imagine boys as writers in totalitarian systems, where direct statements are risky, and to escape sanction they must express feeling in a language that looks very different—often the opposite—from what they intend.

One of my college students, Andrew Schneller, explains this coding in an illuminating account of his literacy experiences in public school. As an eighteen-year-old, Andrew admits he does not enjoy writing and wants to avoid it when he can. But it was not always this way. He describes with considerable detail the pleasure he had writing in the early elementary grades, beginning with his memory of first grade:

> The first day of school that year I met Jon Cortis. Jon would later become my best friend through elementary school, and in junior high we were inseparable. . . . I remember an assignment where we were supposed to draw a picture and write a sentence about it. I drew a shark (I used to spend my summers on the beach and developed a fascination with sharks). John drew a scuba diver covered with missiles and lasers. His sentence was "The underwater trooper kills all the sharks." Not to be upstaged, I decided to add missiles and lasers to my sharks and wrote: "Attack sharks kill underwater troopers." It was a very weak sentence, but I was (and still am) very competitive.
>
> Second grade Jon was in my class again. This year we focused on writing. We had to write a story each week. It seemed that all of Jon's stories were about underwater troopers killing my attack sharks. His stories always ended with a shark named Andrew dying in a different gruesome manner each time. Again I retaliated by having my sharks destroying his troopers, always ending with a trooper named Jon dying some humiliating death.

I suspect that if this writing were subject to the analysis traditionally used in studies of gender, Andrew's and Jon's stories would fit the familiar pattern—violent, competitive, individualistic, devoid of female characters, and from the teacher's standpoint numbingly repetitive. Yet Andrew's stories were intensely social; they helped form and maintain a continuing bond with his best friend. Dyson (1993) coined the term "social work" to describe the "off task" affiliative work that writing does. This work may not be evident in the written product, more often appearing in the talk and negotiation ("Can I be the pilot?") that surrounds the writing. In Andrew's case, seemingly antisocial, "violent" writing performed a positive collaborative function. And these writing experiences remain for him the most enjoyable of his school years.

As Andrew moved through school, he lost the opportunity to make choices about reading and writing, and consequently lost interest in both. But he does cite one other positive experience, in seventh grade, with his underwater opponent Jon:

> That summer we read *Jurassic Park*. It was the first book I read on my own in a long time. I enjoyed it and recommended it to Jon, who also read and enjoyed it. There must be something about dinosaurs ripping people to shreds that appeals to twelve-year-old boys.

Here we see the pattern repeated: A book with sensationalist violence performs real social work, strengthening a bond between friends. After they saw the movie they discussed its differences from the book, finding the book better. Andrew concludes, "I had regained my love of reading."

We can see a similar friendship group at work in "Motorcycle Mice," a story written by fourth grader Jeremy. I reproduce it here in its entirety:

### Motorcycle Mice

There once was five mice named Basil, Jeremy, Seth, Jake, and Russell. Basil was a crazy old mouse on a motorcycle who always took stupid risks. Basil had 1 broken leg, 1 broken arm, and 4 broken fingers! But still he rides his motorcycle. Seth is a kind of mouse that always makes up these funny dances. Jeremy was a mouse who always got in fights and did stupid things. Jake is the kind of mouse that always takes a mouse's jacket without asking! And always steals food. Russell is a mouse that always sits around and shoves cheese up his nose and pops them out and hits us! It hurts a lot. Especially when it hits you on the tail or ear!

One day when Basil, Seth, Jake, Russell and I were riding our motorcycles a cat jumped out behind us. Basil was in front of us. Basil was going so fast that his tail was wandering around so much that it got caught in the spokes of his motorcycle! Snap Basil's tail came right off. Now Basil looks like a hamster. Russell was going really too fast too. Too fast. He was going so fast that when he ran over Basil's tail he crashed. Bye, bye Russell. He got ate by the cat. Everybody was so mad at the cat. They wanted to get him back.

So Jeremy, Basil, Seth, and Jake made a plan to get the cat back. So here's the plan. Jake you go steal some fish from the market. Basil, Seth, and I will distract the cat while you put the fish in the cat's bowl. Then the cat will chase us but she will stop to eat the fish. Then we can go get some mouse traps. When the cat is eating the fish we can sneak up behind her and snap a mousetrap on her tail. Then Danny and Basil come out on your motorcycles and run over the cat's paws. That cat will never bother us again. And she never did. But Basil, Seth, Jake, and I had a funeral for Russell. We invited every mouse. And they came. And all the mice said they would remember Russell for the rest of their lives.

I interviewed Jeremy about the origins of the story. The idea came not from Tom and Jerry cartoons, as I had expected, but from watching his cat stalk his hamster (thus the comparison of tailless Basil to a hamster). Danny, Basil, Russell, and Jake are all friends in his class, and at that time they were all featuring each other in their stories. The idea for making them a motorcycle gang came from Beverly Cleary's *Runaway Ralph*. In Dyson's terms, the piece shows the "dialogic" relationship of multiple worlds—home, friendship groups, possibly cartoons (as models for the action), and established literature. Jeremy is doing something far more complex than mimicking stories drawn from video culture.

While "violent," "Motorcycle Mice" is unmistakably about friendship, as much so as Mandy's tribute to "A Special Person." There is the constant reiteration of the names in the group, more than would be necessary for the story, each repetition affirming the makeup of the team.

This introduction of characters was a standard feature of the group of stories this group of boys wrote, and they typically enjoyed that part as much as the action of the story itself. Here, for example, is part of Seth's opening to his story, where the mice live inside a Barbie house:

> Jake is the kind of mouse who likes to be cool and do tricks in a Little Mermaid car. One day he went off the little girl's brother's motorcycle jump in the car and flipped all around. Jeremy is the kind of mouse who likes to be a couch potato, you know, sit around, eat and watch t.v. while he was eating. His hand was halfway to his mouth with a potato chip. Another time he fell asleep watching t.v. in a chair and tipped back and fell down all the stairs.

When I asked him to pick his favorite part of the story he immediately chose the image of Jeremy falling asleep with the potato chip in the air.

Both Jeremy and Seth coded their affection for their friends in humor that mocked their idiosyncracies. I asked Jeremy about this:

**TN:** Now do you feel like you know the characters in your story?
**JEREMY:** Yeah. Because all those names are real people in my class.
**TN:** But they don't act like themselves in the story?
**JEREMY:** Yeah. Jake took my jacket one time and started wearing it and I couldn't find it. And Seth does these funny touchdown dances. And Basil does crazy stuff.
**TN:** But that thing with the cheese. I don't imagine any of you could pull off that trick?
**JEREMY:** I bet Russell could.

I shared Jeremy's story (and Mandy's) with a group of elementary school teachers, pointing out that Jeremy is employing a *code* for expressing his affection. He is making no direct affirmations, except possibly to Russell (who, after all, is in the cat's stomach). No references to "special friends"—though that is, of course, what they are. Rather, he affirms connection through a reiteration of names, through joint action, and through his mocking introduction of the main characters, most pointedly his taking Jake to task for "borrowing" his jacket without asking.

My point was to show how Russell operates within the "boy code" to show his affiliation with his friends. The teachers, almost all female, pointed out that Mandy was operating in a "girl code." The code allows direct expression of affection, but would not allow the mockery Jeremy employs. A teasing reference to a "borrowed" jacket would be much more likely to be taken badly by a girl being teased. Even if Jake was a little embarrassed by the reference, Jeremy could count on him to "take it," while Mandy could not be similarly confident. Adult men laugh easily at "roasts" where men tease other men; this teasing feels different, maybe more personal, when women are doing it. But there are clearly cultural and racial differences in women's "right" to tease. Geneva Smitherman (2001) notes that "the dozens," a ritualized insulting game in the African American community, is played by both males and females.

It might be argued that the male code that forces boys to express affection through teasing and shared, often violent, action—and not direct expression—is part of the problem. The boy code sets narrow constraints in which boys must construct their relationships; these restraints offer a safety shield, allowing expressions of friendship while protecting the boys from appearing "gay." But to these boys themselves, this code seems far more expansive and pleasurable—it offers abundant opportunities for shared adventure, for ingenuity and humor. In Seth's interview he mentions another story in which one group of boys kidnaps another group:

SETH: All three of them [his friends] are in another story that we get kidnapped by them and Trevor, he's in our class. He's a police officer that gets shot in the head but he's still alive and he gets tied up with us in the van and we start laughing at him and he shoots us.

TN: How did Trevor like being shot in the head?

SETH: (*Laughs*) He didn't like that too much but that's okay.

I take Seth to be saying, "Mr. Newkirk, you don't get it. This is not real. We are having fun. Lighten up."

## When Violence Becomes Uncomfortable

The "violence" of Jeremy's story is not likely to be alarming for most teachers. It is playful, cartoonlike, laced with humorous references to friends. It is difficult to read any hostile intent into Russell's death or any other action in the story. And like the writing of most boys their age, these stories are safely segregated—no girls allowed. But in one fifth-grade class, boys began to ask girls if they could use their names in violent stories, and the girls' willingness, sometimes eagerness, to be involved raises interesting questions of interpretation. I began by asking Amber about how it felt to be arguing with her good friend Erin. The conversation took a surprising turn:

TN: What's it like to have her write about you when there's an argument? Do you like being a character in her story?

AMBER: Yeah, as long as I don't die. In the boys' stories I die.

ERIN: Yeah, I die in all of them.

TN: So the boys put you in their stories.

AMBER: Yeah, they'll ask to put some of us in their stories and then they'll make you die.

TN: How have they killed you off?

**AMBER:** Well, once I was tortured to death and I was blown up, and I froze to death, and I got eaten by a mutant bug.

**ERIN:** Yeah, we're pretty much the same in their stories. We're bugs. Didn't you drown in one of Anthony's stories?

**AMBER:** Yeah. Once I was this guy's girlfriend and nothing really happened to us.

**ERIN:** (*Laughs*) This guy's *girlfriend?*

**AMBER:** Yeah, nothing happened except I lost my leg.

**TN:** Now do you ever put them in your story as revenge?

**ERIN:** In your story you have Corey.

**AMBER:** Yeah, Corey really isn't in the story. He's the brother and he's one of his sister's imaginary friends living in a shoe.

**ERIN:** And he goes, "Ah, you're killing me."

It is certainly possible to read this exchange as an alarming example of male dominance, reflecting the *givenness* of male-on-female violence. Amber and her friends can be viewed as cooperating in a script that, while it may offer temporary social acceptance, perpetuates a profoundly unhealthy attitude toward women. This being the case, one might argue that the teacher should have prohibited the form of name-borrowing.

But another reading is possible. The male "violence" against women might be read as no more hostile than male-on-male violence in Andrew Schneller's underwater trooper stories. Violence may be a code for something else, in this case for the boys to express their interest in particular girls in the class. It may be on a par with the way boys at this age use physical contact like bumping or pushing girls to send messages. For a girl to be asked to have her name used is a sign of status, a way of connecting with boys in the classroom. Erin, in particular, seemed to enjoy and accept this involvement as normal; what shocked her was not that they were killed in stories, but that one boy had worked outside the code and actually cast Amber as a "girlfriend." The classroom teacher was aware of the name-borrowing and the complex role it played in her class. She viewed this use of "violence" as a "boy thing." I asked her what she meant by that.

The boys want to show they're interested in the girls, but
they still want to show they think girls are yucky. So they
show interest by involving them, but they still show they
"don't really like girls" by causing them to die.

In other words, the boys are able to bridge two identities: the seg-
regationist male role that finds girls officially unappealing—and
the young adolescent role that is beginning to find girls truly interesting. By keeping to action stories, ones *without* girlfriends or real
relationships, the boys can avoid territory that might threaten their
standing as "real boys."

This teacher also pointed out that Amber was well liked by
almost all the class, and her regular appearance in boys' stories
was an index of her popularity (though not necessary for that popularity). Allowing her name to be used made the boys' stories
instantly more interesting because classmates were interested in
what would happen to *her*. The written text can act as a ticket for
admission to a social group, particularly useful for some marginalized students. For example, Erin mentions Anthony's story, a
strange and improbable adventure in which Amber drowns. Once
Anthony had permission to use Amber's name, he had an audience that he probably could not have earned without that special
attraction. As the teacher said, "It's like you have Dustin Hoffman
in a movie and it's guaranteed an audience no matter how good it
is." In a way, Amber gave a small gift to Anthony, and this gen-
erosity was characteristic of the attitude that made her popular in
the first place. So, a complex bit of "social work" here.

To read this situation as a pure example of male dominance,
as an example of a casual acceptance of violence against women,
would be to give a particularly literal reading. It seems more likely
that in these stories the young writers use the coded language of
action stories to establish and affirm their interest in each other.
Probably in no other part of the curriculum could this fine-tuned
social work occur, and I would guess that any attempt to close it
down would be seen as an intrusion into the free, hijacked space
these writers have created within the school curriculum.

Karen Gallas notes a similar problem reading the "gross" and aggressive talk of her first- and second-grade boys. She comments on one incident during recess where Tony whispered to a classmate, Ellen, "Your mother squeezes your brains out your ears." Gallas immediately put a stop to this talk, which she saw as an early stage of sexual harassment. But she was puzzled that Ellen herself was not sure if this talk bothers her. In light of this reluctance, Gallas began to reread the scene as more of an attempt to get attention and explore the boundaries of relationships with the opposite sex. Ellen later admitted that she wanted to hear "a tiny bit of it, but not too much." She was reluctant to totally condemn this talk because she and her peers recognize talk like this as a coded overture (Gallas 1998, 75–78). The code itself allows boys to play the double game: They can define themselves against girls (by being gross) *and* show an interest in them.

This does not mean that anything goes in the playground or classroom (only that within limits, this talk and writing allows for some complex social work to occur). Amber's teacher works hard to set reasonable limits, and to have students *use* the violence in clearly thought-out story lines. According to Amber, boys often don't have a story line:

> They just, like, take two sentences getting there and all
> the action happens. And it doesn't go along with the story
> at all.

While none of the teachers in this project had a flat-out prohibition on violence, they tried to help writers develop plausible plots that might build logically toward a conflict. Suspense, not random violence, is the engine for the fictions boys truly like. Paradoxically, for an action story to create suspense the violent action must be suspended, delayed, so the reader has space to feel the scary pleasure of anticipation.

One fourth grader, Andrew, explained to me how the non-action of his story, "The Monster I Saw," was crucial to the effect he wanted. In the first part of the story he has a terrifying experience with a monster that has "huge wings, the sharpest beak, glaring and glowing eyes, huge feathers, and feet the size to grab my dad and I with just one claw." After the narrator tells his dad about the vision, he goes off on his own:

> I went to the dock and jumped on the jet boat that was tied to the dock that we own. I leaned over the side and put my finger in the water. It felt like a spa! Then I forgot about the monster, my dad waiting, and I even forgot I was outside. I was in my own world thinking of fish while my finger was in the water.

He then hears his dad call for help, and the last sentence of the story shows the father being carried away:

> Then I heard some leaves rattling 100 yards away and there I saw it, the monster I saw at my window, flying toward the moon with my dad in its claw.

When I asked Andrew the part *he* liked best in his story he pointed to the scene on the lake *where nothing happened*:

> The part I liked the best is when his fingers are in the water and it's like he's in his own world thinking of fish. Then all of a sudden his dad yells, "Ah, Tom. Help!"

I told him that I was expecting something to grab his fingers when they were in the water.

**TN:** Did you ever imagine a reader would think that?
**ANDREW:** Yeah. I was going to write, "Then the thing flew out of the water and got him with his beak and carried him away." But I wanted it to be scarier. I wanted it to be that Tom never had a clue; he never saw up front what it actually looked like.

And, of course, he's right. It is far scarier for him to be startled out of this dreamworld and watch helplessly as his father is carried away.

## Girls Write Violence

To this point the issue of violence has been presented as predominantly a male concern, yet studies of writing preferences show that horror fiction appeals strongly to both boys and girls. In her analysis of eighty stories written by eleven-year-olds, Elaine Millard (2001) found horror by far the most popular genre for girls, and for boys it was a close second to adventure stories. Christopher Pike and R. L. Stine are immensely popular models in elementary and middle school, leading to Stephen King, Dean Koontz, and Anne Rice for high schoolers. The most detailed violence in the stories I collected came in a horror story written by Carin, a fifth-grade girl. A "seed" in the wall goes off, making the wall lethally magnetic:

> BEEP! Went the seed in Jackie's wall.
>
> "Like shut up Jackie," Candy called from her room.
>
> "Wasn't me," Jackie said innocently. Suddenly Jackie's bookmark flew off from her bed and stuck to the wall. Then all of the small metal things, such as tacks, rings, and necklaces, suddenly flew to the wall and stuck also.
>
> Then Jackie started being pulled. First it was her shoes. Jackie grabbed on to the sheets. Her arms were getting weak because now she was grabbing and scrambling on the sheets for her life. She felt a strong tingling and she was finally flung from her bed and stuck to the wall.
>
> She squinted in pain as the necklaces that she was wearing started cutting into the back of her neck. Her ears started bleeding too as her earrings were also being tugged at by the seed. Her feet had punctured the wall because her bureau pushed hard up against her feet. Jackie's head hurt from the ringing sound that came from the wall.

When I asked Carin and her cowriter, Pam, to pick a part of the story that they liked best, they both picked this section.

**PAM:** Well, I liked all the detail in it. How much her neck hurt because it started bleeding because of her necklaces, and her ears because they were bleeding too. I thought that was descriptive.

**TN:** Going back to an earlier question, a lot of people say boys like writing about violence, but there's a lot of violence here—do you like writing about that stuff?

**CARIN:** Well, I just thought I didn't want it to be a book that didn't have any violence in it because it just isn't that kind of book for me so I thought we should add in things about what Jackie truly felt. So I just opened up my imagination and just scribbled it down quickly. And that's how it came to be.

There seemed to be a vicarious pleasure for Carin in imagining the panic and pain of her main character as the seed in the wall took hold.

Girls' attraction to violence raises a slightly different set of cultural anxieties. If boy's violence "normalizes" the use of force to deal with disputes, girls' violence normalizes their victimhood. In the fictional worlds they enter (through reading *and* writing), females are constantly in danger from stalkers, killers, vampires. To the extent they accept this situation as a given, one might argue that they become complicit in their own victimization. Forms of male aggressiveness can be seen as natural, while vulnerability and fearfulness are the lot of females. On the surface, it seems easier to understand boys' craving for dominance (they can have a power that's denied them in "real life") than it is to understand the well-documented pleasure girls take in vampire stories where they are cast as targets and potential victims.

In an extraordinary set of interviews, Ruth Vinz (1996) asked adolescent girls to discuss their attraction to vampire stories. Many expressed a complex love/hate attitude toward the genre:

> It's like you see something so disgusting that you're temporarily hypnotized by it. It's like that for me in vampire stories. The stories are overpowering. It's like I want to gag at the same time I want to drink them in. (19)

An eighth grader similarly described this conflict of attitudes:

> I get mad and excited all at the same time. The helpless female hits
> a raw nerve. But I like the story line and get caught into it because
> it is so—let's see—it's shocking to be attracted to violence that is
> sexual, but I am, and I can't understand the feeling, but I love to feel
> it. (19)

Vinz in not entirely comfortable with these responses, but she
sees these young women as claiming a transgressive pleasure that
has been traditionally associated with gothic fiction. This literature opened a space in which the "constraints of a fixed social role"
are suspended, where the rules change in fascinating and even
repellant ways:

> In embracing horror, these adolescents embrace possibilities of new
> order, new worlds where they are not confined to their prepubes-
> cent or sexually burgeoning selves, but can rewrite the body of
> desire in ways that free them to explore their own feelings and emo-
> tions within some controlled disorder without fear of repercussion.
> (24)

These stories may allow the reader to feel an illicit pleasure in the
overwhelming physical attraction of the female protagonist.

In many of these horror stories, the protagonist's "safe" sub-
urban community becomes dangerous. Things are not what they
appear to be; authority figures, whose role is to protect and super-
vise, turn threatening. Or, at the very least, they are unable to effectively protect. Even that most comforting of spaces, one's own
bedroom, can become suddenly menacing.

These fictions allow an escape from safety. While adults may
describe the world children face as one of menace and threat, children often see it as one of *not enough threat*. Social critic David
Brooks, in his essay "The Organization Kid" (2001), has described
the intense supervision that has become the norm in middle-class
parenting, a break from a more permissive (or trusting) view of

previous generations. He describes children today as "the most honed and supervised generation in human history." He attributes this intense monitoring to a quiet revolution in parenting, citing among other sources Patricia Hersch's *A Tribe Apart* (1999), an angry rebuke to permissive parents that has this advice:

> The lives of kids in this book illustrate in subtle and not so subtle ways the need for adult presence to help them learn the new lessons of growing up. Kids need adults to bear witness to the details of their lives and count them as something. They require the watchful eyes and community standards that provide greater stability.

Hersch's reference to "watchful eyes" calls up an image that at the time signified to me the fate of the "organization kids" in Durham, New Hampshire. It is a Saturday morning at the local gymnastics center:

A group of eight-year-old girls, my daughter among them, are doing "crunches" in preparation for their lesson. It is a warm day, a beautiful day, and they begin to sweat as the instructor passes through them urging them to work hard and concentrate. The parents stand on a balcony overlooking the exercise area; they are also sweating—and watching everything. So many eyes. Such oppressive "bearing witness." How did we all, on this glorious summer day, end up in this script?

## Jamie: A Case Study in Violent Writing

The Pulitzer Prize–winning poet Charles Simic once noted that there are two kinds of poets—those who create images with their eyes open, and those who create them with their eyes closed. Some gain their descriptive power by paying careful attention to what they see; others, like Simic himself, by focusing their attention on an inner dreamlike landscape. Jamie, a fifth grader in Mike Anderson's class, was clearly a writer who relied on this inner landscape.

At times his inner world seemed more real to him than what was going on about him. On his way to recess, he would be simulating galactic battles with lasers and bullets flying around him. When I asked him how he was able to sustain his long stories, he admitted that he sometimes did lose interest, "but then I stop for a little bit, and then I keep getting pictures in my head and then I think of my story and convert those pictures into the story."

When teachers worry about violence in writing, it is often students like Jamie they have in mind. A reclusive student, obsessed by video games (he claimed to have played them since he was three), his stories are complex series of battles with complex weapons in which a band of friends single-handedly kills off the enemy, both mechanical and human. In "WWIII," a reprise of WWII, the enemy is Japan, which is "nuked" at the end of the story by a bomb that combines fission and fusion. Jamie's favorite creation in "WWIII" is a mechanical scorpion (see Figure 6–1), drawn with loving care, that defends the islands. Here is Jamie's description of the battle:

> There coming right at them was a mechanized scorpion, with pincers that looked as if they were 25 pounds each and a giant whip-like scorpion tail with king cobra venom and several laser cannons. {intruder! intruder!} said the mechanized beast. It walked forward and slammed Matt into the wall with its monstrous claws. Matt was knocked unconscious. Then it pummeled Daron with a laser, Daron couldn't move. "It's just you and me now," said Kujo. Kujo ran up and sliced a leg off the scorpion. The monster rapidly tried to sting Kujo but missed. "Gimme all you got!!!" screamed Kujo.

In retaliation, a robot charged up the huge laser in the eye at the center of the scorpion and fired it at Kujo, killing him. Daron then attacked the scorpion, using his sword to slice the core of the scorpion in half, creating a blinding explosion. In Jamie's media-driven narrative, the mechanized scorpion could be viewed as his most inventive "special effect," and months later, it is the one he is most proud of.

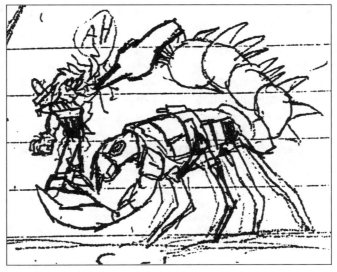

FIGURE 6–1 *Mechanical Scorpion*

In a teacher research project, Jamie's teacher, Mike Anderson, studied the stories Jamie produced. He began by watching one of Jamie's favorite cartoons, *Digimon*. In the cartoon a select group of friends can transport themselves into a digital world, where each is paired with an animal who shares special powers with them and can transform them into semirobotic creatures. Together they fight the evil villain of the digital world. Anderson describes the experience of watching *Digimon*:

> While watching this cartoon I was transported back to my own boyhood when every Saturday morning would be spent watching *Tarzan*, *The Superfriends*, *Dungeons and Dragons*, and *Scooby Doo*. I was struck by the elements of *Digimon* which reminded me of my favorites. First and foremost, the heroes in *Digimon* are children, which makes the story automatically more personal and interesting for kids. There is the classic struggle between good and evil, where kids are battling someone who is out to destroy helpless innocents. The characters have special powers (such as the ability to control wind or fire). (2000)

Anderson was struck by the way these elements also played in great fantasy classics like *The Chronicles of Narnia* and the *Lord of the Rings* trilogy—and in Jamie's own stories like "The Adventure," a story in which two friends are on a mission to Mars and must fight the inevitable giant scorpion, a red-eyed bat-winged creature, and the evil adult character Syrenoth. Intrigued by this similarity, Anderson began to list common elements:

> *Good Versus Evil*: Tom and Mike try to escape from an evil villain to get back to their mission to Mars.

> *Heroes Are Underdogs*: Tom and Mike are constantly outnumbered by overpowering forces, yet manage to escape over and over again.

> *Kid Heroes*: Tom and Mike are battling a more powerful adult.

> *Action/Excitement/Adventure*: Tom and Mike battle giant scorpions, other monsters and soldiers, crash in their spaceship, and face many other dangers.

> *Magical Powers*: Tom and Mike have super powers and weapons which are very attractive to a young boy looking to be special/powerful and have control over the natural world.

> *Friendship*: Tom and Mike are friends in the story, showing this friendship through concerted action. These are also the names of friends in the class. In typical boyish style, the death of Mike at the end of the story may be the ultimate show of friendship.

A story that Anderson might originally have dismissed as a boring rambling video game on paper began "to look more and more like real literature."

While Jamie's stories obviously draw from the visual sources he loves, he is never simply summarizing a single show. To do so would be simply an act of remembering, and writers this age typically do not wanted to be limited to memory as a source (which is, for many, a limitation of personal narratives) (Newkirk 2000). Like Jamie, they mix elements that come from different sources. I interviewed Jamie as he was beginning a story called "The Zarkans Assault" in which humans, now living in floating colonies orbiting around Earth, are attacked by the Zarkans. The idea of floating colonies came from a show he liked watching, *Gundam Wing* (there are more than 270 Yahoo! fan clubs for this program). Jamie's story opens with soldiers racing after a character called the Outlaw, wounding him in the arm. This scene, according to Jamie, came from a dream:

JAMIE: I had a dream that there was this exact guy and he was running away from soldiers. He kept on getting shot. A soldier rescued him, brought him out of the city, found a girl which the soldier knew, the big sister died, and then it shows a replay of what happens. The two of them were in a boat paddling around, and suddenly the water became black, and there were bones in it and then kind of an island, and that was it.

TN: I see. Do you always remember your dreams that carefully?

JAMIE: Only the really good ones like that.

Recalling the dream, Jamie could clearly see both the Outlaw (who resembled Jamie himself) and the soldier:

JAMIE: I don't know where I got the idea for small [for the size of the Outlaw]. It just appeared in the dream and the soldier is really tall and has yellowish, blondish hair, short yellow hair. And this guy [the soldier] wears only black. He has a black leather jacket, black shirt, black eyes, black hair.

TN: You got all that from the dream?

JAMIE: Yeah.

Not only does Jamie recover the dream in cinematic detail, but the dream itself has cinematic structures, specifically a flashback (what Jamie calls a "replay") of an earlier death. Technology has shaped his dream narratives.

When I asked Jamie what made a good story, his first descriptor was "long." His stories are longer than those of any other in the class, and here too there seems to be a connection to the extended contests in his video games. While these games are typically dismissed as a form of instant gratification, catering to the minute attention span of today's children, "beating a game" is a long and detailed process, involving a long series of tests and battles. Jamie boasted of beating Final Fantasy 9 "surprisingly quickly." I asked how quickly that was, and he replied, a month and a half:

TN: Is that fast?

JAMIE: Yeah.

TN: What do you have to do to beat it? What skill does it take for you to beat it?

JAMIE: It takes guessing and being prepared for what is like a really big boss or something. I can feel I am going to fight one so I save the game, build up the guy's levels, save again, and then fight him. So I should be prepared.

TN: So you really have to do a lot of planning for it.

JAMIE: Yeah. And sometimes I just stop and train because there's a certain spell that will come soon and I want to get it. Or I want to increase hit point. You know what I mean?

TN: Kind of.

This is hardly mindless visual stimulation. When I watched my nephews play video games like this one, I was dazzled by the split-second decision making, the calculation, the shifting from mode to mode. When I tried it, I felt like a total bumbler, hopelessly overmatched. While schools promote strategic thinking and problem solving, I imagine that for adept players like Jamie, the video game is a much richer cognitive experience. Michael Smith and Jeffrey Wilhelm (2002) argue that video games have many of the characteristics of optimal learning environments, where the learner enters a "flow state":

- sense of control and competence
- challenge that requires an appropriate level of skill
- clear goals and feedback
- focus on immediate experience

And for Jamie, who spent fourth grade with a child-specific aide hovering over him, who was constantly being sent to the "time out" chair, what mastery and power must come from the steady accumulation of points and finally "beating the game."

The pace of Jamie's stories seems nonstop; the reader experiences his story as an often bewildering sequence of battles, rescues, and transformations. Yet I suspect that Jamie's primary experience of the story is *as a writer*. The adventure that races forward, often incomprehensibly, for us is experienced by him at a slower, writerly pace. The images of mechanical scorpions, which as readers we glance at, may have taken most of a writing period to draw. The story is the product of days, even weeks, of composing, with Jamie playing out events in his mind all the while, even when not writing. His experience of the story is not one of quickness, but of epic length. He is not accommodating the reader, or, I would guess, even imagining the reader. Jamie didn't care whether his writing was shared in class or bound into a book; it was simply tucked in the back of an old folder (it took him *forever* to find it when I interviewed him). When I asked if other kids in the class read his story, he shrugged, "If they wanted to." He was writing almost exclusively for the pleasure of writing. This is *his* space.

In a way, his writing was like much of his classroom behavior: He lacked the self-consciousness of most of his classmates, for whom writing was a gregarious shared experience. While many of them were performing, at least in part, for each other, Jamie was performing for himself. I realize that audience awareness is generally recognized as a necessary capability for the developing writer, and by this standard I suppose Jamie could be viewed as immature. But he clearly has something else at least as valuable—

the world-creating obsessiveness that fiction writers speak of, the capacity to dwell in a created space that seems as real as the tangible world around them.

At the end of our interview, I asked him to respond to the criticisms that have been made about video games and the ways they contribute to violence in student writing.

JAMIE: I do play them a lot, but that actually helps me in my writing, along with TV and stuff. So it's just kind of a good thing.
TN: Because you take ideas from video games and use them?
JAMIE: I take *slight* ideas. That guy—do your remember the guy Seronal from the Earth, the weird guy from the ten-page story that I wrote? There's a guy from Final Fantasy 7 named Seferol. So I kind of built the other guy on Seferol.

I then asked him to confront head-on the issue of violence in writing:

TN: But suppose someone said, "Okay, you can write stories, but can't you write stories where there are no battles or nobody got killed?" Suppose they made that rule. Why wouldn't that be a good rule?
JAMIE: Because it wouldn't. Because then it would be that they're too secure and they [kids] want the story to go anywhere they like. With that rule, they can't.

Puzzled by his use of the word "secure," I went on:

TN: You said "too secure."
JAMIE: That's not exactly what I meant, but you have an idea of what I meant.
TN: "Secure" means "safe" and you don't want to write a story that's too safe?
JAMIE: Or too closed in.

Then he paused and looked at the tiny, claustrophobic conference room where the interview was taking place, padded on the sides with carpet for kids who are literally "off the wall":

JAMIE: For instance, this room. It's kind of small. With that rule it's too closed in. Without that rule they have the space they need. It's how I feel.
TN: And if you didn't have that freedom you wouldn't want to write?
JAMIE: Yeah. "Freedom. Freedom." That's the kind of word I was thinking of.

It is easy, too easy, to see Jamie's love of video games as the sign of a wasted childhood, an addiction that needs to be broken. As we spoke in this tiny room, I thought that maybe we need to take Jamie at his word. He is truly happy and powerful when he plays video games.

In some ways this world of video games is foreign to me, and when I watch a skilled player like Jamie the game moves so fast I almost get nauseated. I am disoriented by the shifts and split-second decision making, and reluctant to break the players' total absorption to ask for explanations. The literary critic George Steiner describes his own sense of being excluded from this world:

> I meet one of these children; I am told he can neither read nor write, or barely; he resents any attempt to pull him away from the screen and make him read. I lose my temper and shout "You are illiterate" because, indeed, I cannot follow what he is doing. If you have watched some of these children, their fingers are like those of a great piano virtuoso. I cannot put this intelligently—their fingers are thinking and creating. The way the fingers move is the way a musician with a motif, or the sketch of a motif or a bar relation, comes back to it through his fingers to reexamine its possibilities and correct it. And the child says I am illiterate. . . . We stare at each other. (1998, 278–79)

Steiner can, of course, argue that *his* view of literacy is the one that counts, the one that will pay dividends in the future—but I suspect he's not so sure.

Yet at the same time there is something deeply familiar about these games, universal story elements. I'll end with my own "final fantasy." I imagine taking one of the Playstation games back to the time when *Beowulf* was still an oral story; I'll travel through one of those time portals kids love to employ in their stories. Once I make my preliminary explanations about electricity, the number system, and the rules of the game (like I said, this is a fantasy), I sit back and watch them play, hesitantly at first, then enthusiastically. A crowd gathers. The day gets late. They build a fire, and I can see the reflections of the flames on the screen. Finally a young boy elbows his way in for a turn, and easily defeats the older men in the group.

Wizards, magic powers, battles, special weapons, powerful villains, quests. It all makes perfect sense to them.

# Making Way for Captain Underpants
## A Chapter in Three Acts

### A Conversation with My Son
ANDY: I can make it to W.

　ME: What? What are you talking about?

ANDY: Burping. I can get to W in a burp. Listen.
　　　(*Demonstration not reducible to print.*)

ANDY: Only K. But I did make it to W. And once I
　　　almost, *almost*, made it the whole way.

　ME: Impressive, Andy. Impressive.

### Act 1: *Dumb and Dumber*—A Trip to the Movies

Humor is an elusive topic. Explain it too much and you kill it. The humor of kids in school is primarily oral and physical, whereas schooling tends to focus on reading and writing. It is primarily subversive, mocking adult authority so that any humor that we propose to "teach" may be too domesticated and sanctioned to appeal to kids. And male humor in particular deals with the body in ways that are designed to make adults uncomfortable—that's part of the point. It flaunts the code of embarrassment or shame; it directly attacks the social conventions that says which body parts must be covered, which bodily acts must be hidden from public view, and which bodily noises must be silenced.

This humor is a field of energy that surrounds what we do in classrooms; it fits into the cracks and open moments in the hallway, before official work begins, during official and self-determined breaks in sanctioned activity. It is the adhesive that connects a generation, more powerful and appealing—more ancient and enduring—than most of the official learning in schools.

The best teachers I know do not want this humor entirely confined to the hallways because they need the energy that comes with it. They allow this humor to enter the official classroom in moments, toned down perhaps, often off the subject, mildly subversive, but working to create community. Just listen to kids talk about teachers they like. They rarely talk about learning in the sober, official ways adults do. Rather, they talk about personality, about appealing strangeness; they describe times when the official world gave way to their culture, or when a teacher stepped out of his role to acknowledge the things that make students laugh.

A few years ago I spent some time looking at middle-school humor. I warmed up for this task by staying up late enough to watch *Beavis and Butt-Head* for a month. But my focus here will be on a trip with my eleven-year-old son, Andy, and his friend to see *Dumb and Dumber*. This movie seems to be some kind of litmus test; it was panned by almost all adult reviewers. Both the *New York Times* and the *Boston Globe* gave it "Don't Bother" ratings. Fortunately for this movie, kids don't read reviews—or, like my older daughter, they find them inversely reliable. *Dumb and Dumber* became the hit of the winter season, grossing over $120 million. I speculated that the people who made this film knew something about their prime audience that the *Boston Globe* and the *New York Times* couldn't figure out. I was right.

On the way to the theatre we picked up my son's friend Sean, a notorious eater and humorist. He brought up a contest he had participated in on a recent school trip to Philadelphia.

"We had a point system. A small one that doesn't smell is one. If it smells, that is two. If it echoes you get five points. And if it echoes *and* smells, that's seven. But most of the ones that echo *do* smell. I was the winner."

"How many did you get?"

"One hundred and forty-two, but they were mostly small ones. Matt had some echoers."

"What were you eating?"

"Fast food."

At the theatre we met another friend, Robert, who greeted us with the news that someone had thrown up in the left aisle. "Whatever you do, don't go down the left aisle." Andy and Sean, of course, went down to take a look.

By the time the three boys, Robert's mother, Susan, and I had taken our seats near the front, it seemed as if we had been *in* the movie for a while. Or more accurately, the movie was a seamless extension of what we had been talking about.

I won't burden you with the plot because the movie doesn't really burden us with one. It's basically a road movie in which Dumb (Jim Carey) and Dumber (Jeff Daniels) drive from Providence to Aspen (once they realize Aspen in not in Florida) in a van that looks like a dog. The trip allows for a series of jokes and gags that cover just about every form of bodily secretion. To even begin to describe these scenes, I realize, may suggest to you that my own sense of humor fixated at a pre–*Mad Magazine* level. But there it is. We all roared.

Since my purpose for this excursion was purely research, I asked Sean and Andy about their favorite parts. Sean picked a joke that Dumber tells at a swank party in Aspen:

"You know, I've done some interesting dog breeding."

"You have?"

"Yes. I once bred a Shih tzu with a bulldog. (*Pause*) We called it a Bullshit."

Daniels convulses in laughter at his own joke, and we join him—

we laugh at the joke, at him telling this joke in this setting, at the guests' uncomfortable laugher, and at ourselves laughing with him.

Andy picked a dream sequence, where Carey imagines himself in Aspen entertaining a group of posh new friends. He finishes one joke and the group erupts. He is on a roll. Then he says, "Now watch this." He sits down, lifts his legs in the air, holds a lighter near his butt, and the next thing we see is the glow of burning gas. The Aspen crowd loves it.

My own favorite comes early in the movie when the two are on the run from an angry trucker, and Carey has to pee. They can't stop, so he fills several empty beer bottles that are lying around in the car (I won't describe the facial expressions of relief). Suddenly an officer pulls them over and sees the beer bottles in the car. "Hand me one!" he says.

Carey and Daniels try to convince him that he really doesn't want these bottles, which only increases the officer's suspicion.

"Hand me one!" They reluctantly comply. The officer slowly brings it to his lips, slowly drinks, and we watch his expression dissolve from arrogance to puzzlement to sickness, and he barely manages a "Get out of here."

Okay, enough. I realize that the type of humor I have described is crude, crass, and vulgar. It is easy to play the part of the disapproving adult we once swore we would never become. But if this humor is vulgar, it is also incredibly enduring; it will still be flourishing long after the whole language movement is forgotten. Even the humor we approve of draws on this more "vulgar" tradition. Roald Dahl's *BFG* plays with taboos about farting, as does Robert Munsch's *Good Families Don't*, as does Cervantes in *Don Quixote*. Shakespeare regularly drew from bawdy street humor in his creation of characters like Falstaff and the nurse in *Romeo and Juliet*.

The greatest humorist of the Renaissance, Francois Rabelais, took special delight in sexual and bodily humor. In his tale *Gargantua*, he describes in detail the making of the codpiece for the giant young hero:

> I call upon God as my witness, if it wasn't a sight worth seeing.
> But I will tell you more about it in the book which I have written,

*On the Dignity of Codpieces.* I will tell you one thing, right here, however, and that is that it was very long and ample, and that it was well furnished and well victualed inside, being in no way like those hypocritical codpieces that a lot of lily-boys wear, which are only filled with wind, to the great detriment of the feminine sex. ([1534] 1946, 74)

In fact, the infant Gargantua's penis was a major topic of conversation among his nurses, who would tie ribbons and tassels around it.

One of them would call it my little spout, another my peg, another my coral branch, another my stopper, my plug, my centerbit, my ramrod, my gimlet, my trinket, my rough-and-ready-stiff-and-steady, my probe, my little red sausage, my little booby prize. (80)

As Philippe Aries ([1962] 1998) has noted, this kind of teasing about infant sexuality was very common at the time.

Gargantua was impressive in other ways. As a young man his solution to a problem set by his father earned him great praise. The task—to determine the best material for wiping your butt (the answer—the neck of a goose). In fact, this probably *was* something people talked about before the days of inexpensive paper.

A couple of generations later, Montaigne criticized a tendency to deny the body:

We seek other conditions because we do not know what is within us. So it is no good mounting on stilts, for even on stilts we have to walk with our own legs; and upon the most exalted throne in the world it is still on our bottoms that we sit. ([1595] 1987, 406)

The body is the great leveler—even kings and queens sit on their butts. The body and its functions are what we have in common, no matter what our social status is. They are "vulgar" in the original sense of the word; they are "common, customary, ordinary."

Montaigne even collected farting stories, as did scholars through the ages, and in his essay on "On the Power of the Imagination" he has this to say:

To show the limitless authority of our wills, Saint Augustine cites the example of a man who could make his behind produce farts whenever he would: Vives [a Spanish scholar] in his glosses goes one better with a contemporary example of a man who could arrange to fart in tune with verses recited to him; but that does not prove the pure obedience of the member, since it is normally most indiscreet and disorderly. In addition I know one Behind so stormy and churlish that it has obliged his master to fart wind constantly and unremittingly for forty years and is thus bringing him to his death. ([1595] 1987, 115–16)

It would be difficult to imagine today a high Catholic churchman, let alone one destined for sainthood, collecting farting stories. All of which suggests that for all of the exhibitionism of our age, we may be more squeamish and secretive than people in previous eras were.

This humanistic view of the human body remains profoundly subversive to a large section of the American public. Despite the so-called sexual revolution, MTV, and talk shows, we live in a culture that regularly makes us uncomfortable about our bodies and what gives us physical pleasure. The mechanism for attacking this humanistic view is, of course, shame and self-consciousness. Take for example the lesson that boys learn early: After peeing, you should wash your hands. *Always.* It doesn't matter if you didn't pee on them, because the part of the body you touch is inherently dirty. No matter how technically clean your penis is, your hands become dirty by touching it, automatically. I was explaining this practice to a woman I know and she said, "You'd think boys would be taught to wash their hands *before* peeing." What a different message that would send!

Or take body odor. Anyone who has spent time in the later elementary- and middle-school grades notices that boys in particular begin to sweat and smell. In middle school, Andy and his friends got the body odor lecture in health, and they were informed of the powers of deodorant. For about a week there was a run on Mennen Speedstick at the local drugstore, and they'd coat their hairless underarms (though most didn't keep it up). Again, the message is: Your body's natural functions are socially inappropriate.

Or take the language we use to describe menstrual products. I remember as a kid hearing the term "sanitary napkin." I knew the meaning of both words, but it literally took me *years* to figure out what it was. Surely any product that needs such a euphemism must serve a secret, and personally shameful, bodily function. At least that seemed to be the cultural message being sent.

I could multiply these examples (e.g., the way girls and women dress in stalls) that stigmatize the body. The cumulative effect of all these taboos and secretive practices is, as Freud claims, internal tension caused by the suppression. One form of temporary release from the code of shame is sexual and bodily humor, even of the Beavis and Butt-Head variety.

*Beavis and Butt-Head* features two high school losers who spend their time avoiding school, watching MTV music videos, and dreaming about being cool and scoring with "chicks." In some ways they resemble their middle-school audience that watches (and makes fun of) music videos. But they are *so* clueless, and so alienated from school and adult culture, that they live outside the code of shame or embarrassment; in fact, they flaunt that code by introducing the body in situations where it doesn't belong.

In one episode, President Clinton is coming to their school and the principal pays Beavis and Butt-Head $50 not to attend school that day. They never make it out of the school, and during the question-and-answer session they go up to the microphone to ask Clinton a question about his sex life. But before they ask the question, they check out the sound system: "Testicles, testicles, one, two, three."

In another episode, they cut school and walk into what they think is a mall. It turns out to be a business, and they are taken for the "temps." They play along, and are shown the computers and copying machines they will be working with. Beavis types random numbers and letters until the computer overheats and burns. Butt-Head sits on the photographic plate of the copying machine and makes copies of his butt. Later, when customers come in to the company, he greets them with, "Here, would you like a picture of my butt?"

In this brief scene, our heroes defy two essential adult codes: they intrude the body into this overly polite company culture and they defy the code of literacy, the "respect for the written word" that is central to the schoolwork they are skipping and to the quasi-schoolwork of this office. They use machines of literacy—designed for generating and multiplying words—for nonliteracy purposes. Butt-Head deftly substitutes the image of an illicit body part for written language.

It is hardly surprising that bodily humor should be especially popular among middle-school students, who find their own bodies changing by the week. They are, after all, learning our culture's code of embarrassment. At worst, they are learning that their sexuality is "dirty" and literally unspeakable. Humor is a way to subvert these social conventions by watching someone who can flaunt the code of embarrassment. It is also a way of leveling the playing field; teachers and administrators, like kings and queens, all have bodies.

So there we were at *Dumb and Dumber*. I was sitting between my son and a woman I barely knew. Near the end of the movie, Carey, in an act of revenge, puts Ex-Lax in Daniels' drink before he goes on a date. Several minutes later, we see the effects taking hold. His body starts to make noises, hollow sounds that seem to start in his head and move toward his bowels. Daniels looks startled. He rushes around to find a toilet (which he later learns can't flush). He pulls his pants down and relieves himself, his eyes looking upward in prayerful relief.

The boys are laughing madly. I think to myself, "I'm sitting next to a woman I've met only at school bake sales, a woman who always struck me as being refined and sophisticated, watching a man with almost terminal diarrhea."

After the movie, Andy and Sean proclaim it "great" and Robert says it's the best movie he's seen.

And, as we leave the theatre, Susan is wiping tears from her eyes. We agree that the beer bottle scene was priceless.

## Act 2: Humor as Underlife

Devin Bencks, my son's best friend, has spent so much time at our house that for a while he would put items on the shopping list ("Heah, Mr. Newkirk, how about some Cool Ranch Doritos?"). Around sixth grade he developed an imaginary friend, Ed. If you asked Devin a question, like if the Red Sox would make the play-offs, he'd say, "I don't know, I'll have to talk to Ed." When the time came for the state sixth-grade tests, Devin and the rest of New Hampshire's sixth graders were required to imagine they could be anyone for a day, and to write a story about their day as that person. Devin found this assignment "cheesy," calling for a predictable kind of hero worship which he was not about to give in to. The very act of writing for a distant examining body provoked his resistance. "They don't care who I admire; they just want to see if I can write, sentences, periods, that kind of stuff." So he wrote about Ed.

> If I could be anyone for a day, I would be Ed because he is so cool and he rules. If I was Ed I would wake up on a bed of nails sur-rounded by fire. I would then use my rat Binki's saliva to extinguish the flames.

He goes on to spend an afternoon dancing with Whitney Hous-ton, later renting a herd of goats and finally riding off with McNeill (of the *McNeill/Lehrer Newshour*) "into the sunset with our goats." In fact, Devin memorized his essay and turned it into a perform-ance that three years later he could still do upon request.

While at first glance this assignment might seem nonideolog-ical (students can choose any person), I suspect that Devin found it unappealing for several reasons. The assignment suggests that the primary attitude of the writer should be open respectfulness, directed most likely to a member of his parents' (or grandparents') generation. In other words, the assignment subtly calls upon the writer to "identify with the interests of those with power over him—parents, teachers, doctors, public authorities" (Pratt 1996). At the very least, it requires him to identify with the authorities giving the test. Even to write about Martin Luther King Jr. in this context is to play the good student, dutifully respectful of a cultural icon, something Devin was unwilling to do. So he chose parody, a form of calculated resistance that went to the very edge of acceptability.

Humor, and particular parody, is not simply a genre coexisting innocently with other genres. It is a tool for those who feel themselves in a subordinate position; to the extent that those in authority must exert their authority through kinds of discourse (speeches, rules, forms, advice, "good literature"), they leave themselves open to the mockery of these language forms. And as Erving Goffman has argued (1961), even those who generally support the work of an institution must find ways of occasionally distancing themselves from it, to avoid the impression that they are *overidentified*. Even the president of the United States must be able to on occasion ridicule himself, in order to show that he is not wholly invested in his position, that he retains some aspects of *self* in reserve. Goffman astutely notes that those who cannot accomplish this distancing become something of an embarrassment to the institutions that they doggedly serve.

Boys' love of parody and controlled resistance might be viewed as an example of what Goffman calls "underlife." He argues that institutions project an official view of what participants should be putting into, and getting out of, institutions, "what sort of self and world they are to accept for themselves" (304). Here, for example, is one middle-school teacher's description of this official student role:

> Well, it consists of, first of all, to be able to follow directions. Any directions that I give. Whether it's get this out, whether it's put this away, whether it's turn to this page or whatever, they follow it, and they come in and they're ready to work and they know what they're here for. Behaviorally, they're appropriate all day long. When it's time for them to listen, they listen. The way I see it, by sixth grade,

the ideal student is one who can sit and listen and learn—work with
their peers, and take responsibility on themselves and understand
what is next, what is expected of them. (Ferguson 2000, 91)

While this kind of obedience can be gratifying for the teacher,
Goffman would argue that any student so acquiescent to the
demands of the school pays a terrific price. For students, inmates,
or employees to completely accept "the embrace of the institution" is to lose a sense of self. An African American student so
identified with school might be viewed by peers as embracing
whiteness, as denying racial identity.

In the mental hospital where Goffman did his observations,
small acts of rebellion (silence, refusal to take pills, mockery of
aides) constituted an underlife, an attempt by the individual to
"keep some distance, some elbow room, between himself and that
with which others think he should be identified" (319). Goffman,
in my view, explains the tensions we all feel as members of institutions: We feel a need to mock procedures or personality traits of
superiors while at the same time being loyal, even dependent on
that institution for a sense of social identity. We *must*, on occasion,
step out of the role of dutiful employee or student—or risk losing
a sense of selfhood.

Boys are often in the difficult position of maintaining their
standing as sons and students while at the same time distancing
themselves from "sincere" behaviors and language that they see
as threatening and "overidentifying." Parody is one way of meeting *both* these demands. Devin's Ed story is a rejection of the sin-
cerity demand of the state assignment—yet it is also an
identifiable genre that the evaluators recognized. So he was able
to pull off the coup of mocking the assignment *and* getting a
higher score than almost all of those who chose to take it seriously
(such as my son, who wrote on Cal Ripken Jr.).

We can see this balancing act in another piece, cowritten
by Devin and my son in third grade. Devin and Andy wrote
a progress report for their teacher, John (Jack) Callahan. The
report contains some inside jokes (the reference to an "ircele

imitation"—Steve Urkel was a popular and funny TV character at the time); Nabu was an imaginary character Jack invented to teach a math unit—when the unit was over, Jack told students that Nabu died. Here's the report:

> John Richard Callahan
> Progress Report
> Date 2/6/93
> Newkirk/Bencks

> Jack is suffering since his good friend Nabu died. I think his donut cholesterol has gone up since. It has been affecting his work. I think he has donitides. I think he should be tutorhood and I think I found the person that would be perfect for jack madonna. I've talked to madonna and jack will meet her at 3:11 at wiconsin's bingo parlor she'll be wearing her Vogue uniform. I've heard they've made a new dunken donuts at _____. I think jack should take summer school because he needs to work on his cursive sevens. I think he should install a toilet in the room. We have not been able to see a successful ircele imitation if by the end of the week he doesn't do the imitation he will be exspeleed.

> This is the marking of how aubknockshis your sin has been this half year

The boys construct an elaborate rating system and then conclude:

> I hope you are plaesed with what we've written. So now you know how poor a student jack is. I hope you can get jack back on track.

> Sincerely Mr. Newkirk/Mr. Bencks

In this progress report, the two boys were both resisting and embracing the institution of school—or rather, they were embracing *by* resisting. They take on the language of authority and admonition, the presumption to rank, even the prerogative to threaten. They skate close to potentially sensitive areas dealing with the body, Jack's affection for donuts and by implication his concern for his weight; and they introduce the subject of sexuality, arranging the rendezvous with Madonna at the Wisconsin Bingo Parlor. Yet their "progress report" is an unmistakable expression of affection, and it's difficult to imagine a more effective vehicle.

Boys also enjoy writing parodies of well-known stories, "fracturing" them in odd and interesting ways. Eric and Jimmy, both fourth graders, used *Tikki Tikki Tembo*, itself a fractured story of rescue, as the base for their parody. They retain major elements of the story: Tikki's wonderful long name, the brothers playing near a well, and the need to get help for Tikki falling into the well. But they add a character, the Fat Old Guy, who helps the first time Tikki falls; after the second fall, Eric and Jimmy take us into a whole other story:

**N (NARRATOR):** A week passes and **Tiki Tiki tembo no saurenbo cherey berry roachie pip parry pembo** and The Kid were playing baseball by an old well (very stupidly).

**THE KID:** "Pitch the ball, I'm ready!"

**BAT: Crack!**

**TIKI:** "I've got it! I'm falling into a well! Ahhhhhhhhhhhhhhhhhh hhhhhhhhhhhhh."

**THE KID:** "He don't got it!"

**NARRATOR:** The Kid ran up the hill to get the Fat Old Guy. Instead he found a small old guy with a black and white striped coat and hat.

**THE KID:** "Help! My brother **Tiki tiki tembo no saurembo cherry berry roachie pip parry pembo** fell in a well. I need a ladder to get him out!"

**R:** "Hey your brother has a pretty weird name just like mine. Wanna guess it?"

**THE KID:** "No."

**R:** "Oh come on. Do you think it's Chester?"

**THE KID:** "Just give me a ladder."

**R:** "I don't got a ladder but I can spin straw into gold."

THE KID: "We don't have any straw."

R: "Want to ride on my magic cooking spoon?"

They ride on the magic spoon, then crash land near the well, where they see something in the sky:

THE KID: "It's a bird."

R: "It's a plane."

THE KID AND R: "No! It's Dumbo the flying elephant!"

Dumbo splashes into the well, sending Tikki flying out. He hits his head when he lands and is knocked unconscious, forcing Rumpel- stiltskin to whack him with a cooking spoon to bring him back. When Tikki stirs to life, the Kid remarks, "He's back."

Eric and Jimmy use the original *Tikki* story as a scaffold, then overwhelm the plot with the introduction of Rumpelstiltskin (also a story about complicated names)—then add references to Superman, Dumbo, and the *Nightmare on Elm Street* series. As I read it I thought of the "Fractured Fairytales" segments on the old *Rocky and Bullwinkle* shows, that great home of parody for my own generation.

Their love of silly names was shared by so many of the chil- dren I interviewed that I began to see naming as a major form of characterization. One fourth grader said she begins her stories by thinking up the names of characters. One attraction of the great Pokémon phenomenon of the 1990s was clever names like Pikachu; the same could be said for the Teenage Mutant Ninja Turtles of the late 1980s, named after Renaissance painters. Once they came up with good names, they didn't want to lose them. In one interview I asked a pair of third-grade girls if any of the char- acters in their pet adventure series ever died in fights.

ABBY: I didn't want it to be bloody or anything because we still wanted to have the characters. We still wanted to have Fluffy, Mousinator, and Claws because that's why we didn't kill them. Otherwise we'd have to make up new characters. *It would be hard to think of the names.*

Many share Jamie's attitude when he interrupted the reading of his own story to exclaim, "I love weird names."

Matt, a fourth grader and the originator of the Junk Food Ant series, was also a lover of wordplay and visual humor. His story "Moo Moo and Bessie" originated in a trip to Virginia, where he saw a billboard with two cows reading a paper with the headline "Eat Moo Chicken." Here is the story:

> One day two old cows names Moo Moo and Bessie went to a beef manufacturer. It was easy to get them in the truck. But when they got there they weren't so easy to handle after they saw the slicer so the cows ran away.
>
> Thursday 4:00
>
> Moo Moo and Bessie were walking down the road when they saw a sign painter. Moo Moo said, "Moo." When the sign painter saw the cows he ran off the side of the sign and landed in a bush. After that Bessie had a smart idea to take the leftover paint and write eat more chicken. So that they can save the other cows from becoming dead beef. So they climbed up the ladder so they can get to the top of the sign. When they got to the top, Bessie climbed on Moo Moo's shoulders and wrote the sign.
>
> The End

At the end of his story he drew a picture of the two cows painting the sign (Figure 7–1), all built on Matt's fascination with linguistic play, on the *moo/more/moore* being near homophones.

I posed the idea to Matt that I could write a sequel:

**TN:** Yeah, I'm going to write a story where a chicken escapes from a chicken farm and goes and repaints the sign, "Eat Moo Beef."

**MATT:** And they're going to get into a big fight.

**DIDI:** The bull comes and then a rooster comes and they make friends and they take down the sign and put up "Eat Moo Turkey."

**MATT** (*Laughs*): "Eat more people."

**DIDI:** Yeah, "Eat more people."

FIGURE 7–1 *Eat Moore Chicken*

They like the twist they've given the story.

In many cases, an action or horror story becomes a frame for inserting humor, in the same way that action movies like those in the *Lethal Weapon* series do. And when asked to point out the parts of the stories they like best, boys regularly cite these comic spots, often no more than one-liners. In "George and Buff," Billy pointed to this bit of dialogue and description involving the meeting of the narrator, a human named Dan, with a couple of talking rats, George and his bodyguard, Buff:

> "I—I'm Dan," I told him.
>
> "Well," he said, "this is my body guard."
>
> "I'm Buff," the body guard said.
>
> "I can see that," I replied. Buff had a very deep voice. He was also pretty buff.
>
> I had a long conversation with George. Then I got a phone call from the bank. I'm getting the interview for the job I wanted! I danced around, kissed George, stopped dancing and spit.

Comic passages like this one, though only a part of a longer story, draw audience response from both boys and girls. They serve as punchlines, and in rereadings these parts become anticipated highlights. One middle-school student, a reluctant writer, refused to make a list of topics that interested him, and grudgingly listed "The top five things I hate" ("writing" was *both* number one and number two). Third on his list was "the little pool of saliva in the fountain," on which he wrote the following:

> The pool of saliva in the fountain always grosses me out. Its always in your face, all bubley like a pool of molten lava, except its white. Everytime someone drinks from it, more goes in, the closer you are to it the more goes in. If you accidentally spit up water, its all cleared out and it gets more filled in.

This vivid piece of "gross out" description became a hit with his class.

In a collaborative time-travel story, the authors selected one description as their favorite part, showing the stupidity of one of the main characters:

Joe's face looked like his brain was sucked out his head.

"Huh," Joe said dumbly.

"Because we have to save Charles and Max. That's why," Fred snapped.

"Huh okay, " Joe said dumbly.

This group felt that their comedy needed the frame of an adventure story in order to have a plot; and an adventure story needed comedy to maintain reader interest. Jake and Rob explained the mixture in this way:

JAKE: So it [comedy] makes it like they're really interested in it. So, like, it's part horror and part comedy, so they get interested in it.

TN: So the humor gets you interested in the horror.

ROB: Yeah, they go pretty well together. Like the comedy.

Then Jake made a comparison to the Three Stooges films that all of the boys liked, and were obviously imitating:

JAKE: And that's sort of like the Three Stooges—they have a lot of comedy and, like, there's one show with horror in it— they're scared of this graveyard because the body keeps coming up out of it—sort of horror and comedy.

I had never thought of the Three Stooges as involving horror at all, but Jake perceptively noted how their humor operates within established adventure plots (a lot of haunted houses).

## Act 3: Wedgie Power

Dav Pilkey, according to his online cartoon biography, was a class clown in third grade who still holds the record for most crayons up the nose. He claims that he regularly spent time in the hall, where he came up with the idea for a cartoon featuring Captain

Underpants, a principal-turned-superhero who flies around with a red cape and tight-fitting cotton briefs. His teacher warned him that he better get serious because "you can't spend the rest of your life making silly books." But Pilkey admits he wasn't a good listener.

At present, there are five books in the series:

*The Adventures of Captain Underpants*

*Captain Underpants and the Attack of the Talking Toilets*

*Captain Underpants and the Invasion of the Incredibly Naughty Cafeteria Ladies from Outer Space (and the Subsequent Assault of the Equally Evil Lunchroom Zombie Nerds)*

*Captain Underpants and the Perilous Plot of Professor Poopypants*

*Captain Underpants and the Wrath of the Wicked Wedgie Woman*

The first four come in a boxed set with a complementary whoopie cushion (check it out). Pilkey's books have attracted thousands of reluctant readers, mostly boys, into the literacy club by employing bodily humor (lots of references to underwear and wedgies), by satirizing school culture and authorities, by using silly and slightly scatological names, all in an easy-to-read comic-book format. And for all his great silliness, Pilkey overtly challenges the censorious attitude that would keep his books out of the hands of children.

The series features two friends, George Beard and Harold Hutchins, pranksters and class clowns, who have, of course, been examined by school specialists:

> Their guidance counselor Mr. Rected thought the boys suffered from A.D.D. The school psychologist, Miss Labler, diagnosed them as A.D.H.D. And their mean old principal, Mr. Krupp, thought they were just plain **B.A.D.** (2000, 14)

The two boys are marginalized in the school; they are not members of established clubs or groups—in fact, these high-status groups (the football team, cheerleaders) are the object of one of their pranks.

In *Captain Underpants and the Perilous Plot of Professor Poopypants*, the boys get in trouble after adjusting the school sign to "Please Don't Fart in a Diaper." They are excluded from a field trip (to a pizza parlor/video arcade) then teased (by teachers!) for missing out. Like the young Pilkey, these boys' primary interest was creating the subversive Captain Underpants comics that they then photocopied when the school secretary was distracted and sold after school. While the appeal of the Captain Underpants series extends beyond any one group (or gender), Pilkey clearly wants to attract disaffected boys who enjoy silliness, word play, bodily humor, and drawing.

The plots of these stories borrow elements of Superman, with Captain Underpants willing to fight for "Truth, Justice, and *all* that is pre-shrunk and cottony." His super-strength is "wedgie power," and in the first episode he captures the villain by using a set of briefs as a slingshot. But unlike most superhero stories, Mr. Krupp, the principal, cannot choose to transform into Captain Underpants—even the boys, like Dr. Frankenstein, don't understand the transformation (it's caused by a magic ring they bought), and they must struggle to control their creation.

As I read these stories, I felt like I was back with *Mad Magazine* at its laugh-aloud best. Pilkey, of course, knows the immediate appeal of even a reference to underwear, diapers, poop, wedgies, or toilets. He knows the appeal of silly names (recall Eric's story), and in one story the mad scientist forces the entire world to take on silly names and gives a chart for constructing them. Pilkey's name becomes Gidget Hamsterbrains; mine is Falafel Rhinobutt. At one point in this story George (alias Fluffy Toiletnose) uses Professor Poopypants' enlarging machine to restore Captain Underpants (who had become invisibly small) to normal size. With the good captain on Harold's (Cheeseball Wafflefanny's) finger he activates the machine, enlarging the captain but also making Harold's right hand bigger than he is: "The good news was that Captain Underpants had grown larger and was now visible. The bad news was, well, let's just say that Cheeseball was going to have an awful hard time picking his nose with his right hand from now on" (2000, 117).

Pilkey finds ready targets in school culture to mock. On "Stinky Taco Surprise" day, the discarded meals transmute into "The Inedible Hulk," which begins eating everything in sight. A student exclaims, "Help, the Inedible Hulk just ate up 15 folding chairs and the gym teacher." The principal responds, "Oh, no, not the folding chairs." Captain Underpants arrives at the scene, sling-shotting underwear into the Hulk's mouth, only to find the monster likes that as much as the leftover Taco Surprise. He then chases Captain Underpants into the bathroom, where he takes a drink out of the toilet and is flushed down by our hero. In addition to the bathroom humor, Pilkey targets school lunches and the tendency of some administrators to be more concerned about property than people.

Stories build to the requisite deciding battle, which Pilkey prefaces with ironic warnings. In *The Adventures of Captain Underpants*, Harold and George must confront two evil robots, and Harold worries aloud, "We're not going to have to resort to extreme graphic violence, are we?" George replies that he hopes not. The next chapter is titled "The Extremely Graphic Violence Chapter," and it begins with a warning label:

**Warning**

The following chapter contains graphic scenes showing two boys beating the tar out of a couple of robots.

If you have high blood pressure, or faint at the sight of motor oil, we strongly encourage you to take better care of yourself and stop being such a baby.

It's as close as Pilkey gets to addressing what he sees as a censorious attitude that underestimates young readers.

Despite the general praise for this series from librarians and parents, there is naturally an undercurrent of criticism. One mother writes this review at Amazon.com:

My son thought this book was hilarious, and I think most kids would . . . so I am hesitant to criticize anything that encourages kids to read so much. But the fact is I don't want my son growing up thinking it's "cool" or "fun" to pull pranks on other people like the main characters in this book do; I also want them to understand that people such as principals do need to be shown respect, even if one doesn't particularly like them. So because of that I'm not going to get other books in the series.

This is essentially the same concern addressed in the chapters on violence: that children will read the books literally as models for their own behavior.

Here is a response: Boys will read *Captain Underpants*, but not to find real-life models to imitate any more than my generation wanted to literally imitate *The Little Rascals*. The attraction of this form of parody comes out of a sense of power imbalance: Even in the most benign school, students are controlled by adults. Time, space, speaking rights, choice of activities—all are ultimately controlled by those in power. And sometimes this control is not so benign. To be completely compliant is psychologically dangerous, for in overidentification we lose a sense of self; we *become* the institution. Mockery is a necessary form of underlife, a way of resisting the full embrace of the institution, even if we are fundamentally loyal to that institution.

Humor, to be sure, is not always benign—it does, after all, have a target. As Freud claimed, humor can be a form of aggression, working to undermine or disrupt the climate of a classroom. Timothy Lensmire (1994) describes his own decision to censor a piece of writing, "The Zit Fit: Lovers in School," written by one of his third graders. In the story Maya places a classmate, Jil, in a story where she wants to get zits in order to win over a boy who already has zits (she succeeds). Lensmire saw this treatment of Jil—attributing to her this desire for disfigurement—as belittling, and refused to allow Maya to share it with the class. It crossed the line that separates playfulness and mean-spiritedness.

Children can cross these lines, just as adults can. (How many political careers have ended because of an inappropriate joke?) Yet the possibility of abuse cannot obscure the fact the humor, managed effectively, is the gold standard in children's writing. It brings celebrity, its appeal (unlike that of much violence) crossing gender lines. It provides a forum for negotiating and sustaining male friendships, and of making overtures to girls. It allows us all to laugh at the peculiarities of our bodies, as we escape, if only briefly, from our embarrassment at the sounds they involuntarily make and the smells they produce. And when directed at figures of authority, it can provide a sense of agency to those who lack power.

When I hear my son's laugh, a genetic echo of my own, coming out of his room, I know that *Jackass* is on. It's one of his favorite shows, a series of the grossest, most improbable, most self-destructive stunts—two guys spraying each other with pepper spray, rolling a portable toilet down a hill while one of them is inside filming as the shit splatters the walls—and *him*. Then there is "urban kayaking," the times they ride their kayaks down the steps of public buildings or in park fountains. Or the time one of them had both his arms in casts, straight out from his body; and he had to plead with bystanders to please, *please* help him unzip his fly because he had to go to the bathroom. It's as if you imagined the wildest dare-takers you ever met and gathered them to brainstorm together.

"Heah, wouldn't it be fun to be attacked by a Rottweiler?"

"Cool."

"How about riding a tricycle off a roof into a bush?"

"Neat."

I can barely watch. "No, dad, come on, you've got to see this one." I'd love to have this bonding moment, but I wince as these young men hurt themselves, as they blink the pepper spray out of their eyes. One of my university friends has speculated that boys love these shows because they return "sports" to a free form of play, without scores, referees, rules. I try this explanation on Andy.

"You know, you guys think too much."

Often he will multitask, shift his attention from *Jackass* to the fifty or sixty pages of *Jane Eyre* or *Grapes of Wrath* that he must read for the night: a fascinating collage of Mr. Rochester and Tom Joad and urban kayaking. I think that Brontë and Steinbeck once had the power to shock as well, but they seem safely, and irrelevantly, "classic" to Andy.

On the downstairs television I randomly come to a documentary on early barnstormers, amazing clips of biplanes flying under the arches of bridges, of men standing on the wings of planes in flight, of crashing into barns. The similarity strikes me at once.

But the stars of *Jackass* are not really imitating earlier risk takers; they seem to be parodying them, feeding our appetite for mockery. It is easy to imagine one of these urban kayakers strapping on old aviator goggles as he sets out to cascade down the steps of City Hall.

# CHAPTER EIGHT

# A Big Enough Room

The newspaper articles . . . about the upcoming Senate investigation into comic books always cited "escapism" among the litany of injurious consequences of their reading, and dwelled on the pernicious effect, on young minds, of satisfying the desire to escape. As if there could be any more noble and necessary service in life.

—From *The Amazing Adventures of Kavalier and Clay,* by Michael Chabon

In this final chapter, I hope to suggest some practical implications for teaching. These will not be fully tested, failsafe ways of engaging boys (I don't think those exist). Rather they will be what I hope are plausible ideas for opening up the literacy curriculum to make it more appealing for boys—and I hope for girls as well.

The central argument of this book runs something like this: Boys underperform girls in school literacy tasks, but not because they are biologically "less verbal." This would be an essentialist claim, locating "difference" in unchanging human nature—which is not to say that many boys don't accept this explanation. As one of my college freshmen told me (told *me!*), he saw reading and writing as "girl things." It was a matter of X and Y chromosomes. Real men, he may have been saying, have better things to do than read or write.

I suspect that many young boys have internalized this model before they even come to school. The research suggests that they rarely see adult males reading extended fiction (or doing any writing)—and in schools it is the reading of extended fiction that typically marks them as successful readers, even as successful students. Those teachers promoting reading and writing will typically be female, so there is little to challenge a perception of literacy tasks as feminized. I have argued that this problem—this construction of literacy as feminized—cannot be countered if schools fail to be self-critical about what counts and does not count as valid literacy activity. In the end, a broadening of the literacy spectrum will not only benefit boys; it will benefit *any student* whose primary affiliation is to the "low status" popular narratives of television, movies, comics, humor, sports pages, and plot-driven fiction.

## Widen the Circle

The central challenge for schools can be illustrated by the concentric circles of Figure 8–1. The larger circle represents all the forms of narrative pleasure that can be experienced in a culture; they could be written, oral, visual, musical, or, most likely, some combination. It contains rock videos, Web pages, animated cartoons, and gossip. It includes the spectrum of written narratives from low culture (e.g., jokebooks) to acknowledged classics. It even includes narratives (pornography, racist jokes, movies that demean women) that, although legally protected "speech," are clearly pernicious.

The smaller inner circle represents school-sanctioned narratives, those that *count* as a measure of reading and writing devel-

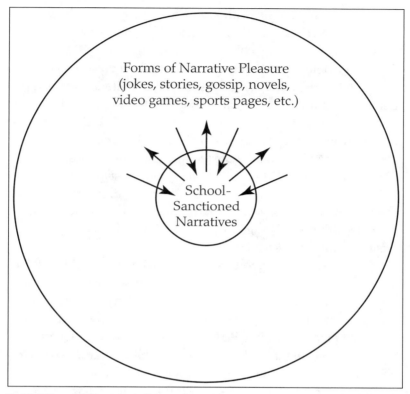

Forms of Narrative Pleasure
(jokes, stories, gossip, novels,
video games, sports pages, etc.)

School-
Sanctioned
Narratives

FIGURE 8–1 *The Permeable Curriculum*

opment in schools. This circle cannot—and should not—be as
comprehensive as the larger circle. Traditionally it focuses on print
literacy, on a literary canon featuring works of high "cultural capital." As I have argued, there is a bias toward a type of fiction that
has thematic weight, that features introspection and the expression of feeling, that engages readers with significant moral issues,
and that helps promote a tolerance for diversity. Preference is
given to books that are morally functional, that assist personal
development and socialization. Books trump magazines; print
trumps the visual; the serious trumps the humorous; fiction
trumps nonfiction. In some cases, literacy instruction is seen as
assaulted on all sides by an indulgent popular culture that now

caters to young people without asking anything of them. The inner circle becomes a wall, a barrier keeping out a degraded, demeaning, and amoral culture (read: MTV).

But I would argue that the more tightly we draw the circle of acceptability, the more students are left out. If literacy instruction defines itself *against* these more popular forms of narrative, we lose a resource, a lever, a connection. As Anne Haas Dyson has so brilliantly argued, the issue is not simply widening the circle; we are not just bringing in this outer culture unchanged. Dyson (1997) argues for a "permeable curriculum" where these popular culture affiliations form the cultural material that children employ (and transform) in their stories. Jamie, the video game fanatic of Chapter 6, used his knowledge of Japanese-inspired video games to create complex *written* adventures.

Jamie provides a good example of what we might call the *obsession theory of writing development*. Literacy development is dependent upon obsessive interests, ones strong enough to sustain the writer in the often-laborious task of developing an extended piece of writing. Writing becomes a way of documenting and employing this allegiance; it piggybacks on these primary affiliations children bring to school. A Red Sox fan may never like writing better than he likes Pedro Martinez, but reading and writing can attest to that allegiance. In some cases, children are affiliated with the "high capital" experiences that align them well with school literacy; they've heard *The Hungry Caterpillar* so often they know it by heart. They have a rich array of experiences to draw on—ballet lessons, trips to the White Mountains, visits to Boston and New York. Others, like Jamie, must rely on "low capital" obsessions, like video games, that may be just as useful in bringing them into the "literacy club."

But accepting this "low capital" material will require us all to imagine a positive role for television programs we rarely choose to watch. I'm always struck by the reaction to statistics about TV viewing among African American and Hispanic children: The call is *always* "How can we get them away from the television set?" In effect, how can they change their lifestyle to be more like white middle-class kids? It's as if there is nothing usable in that TV watching, no possible transfer between these visual narratives and the writing kids might do in school. As if "plot" or "conflict" or "dialogue" on a TV show has nothing to do with writing (even though screen*writers* develop these shows). But if we are to help students *use* these resources, we will need to spend some time with them, maybe watching a few mornings of Saturday *anime* cartoons, a few minutes of Tom Green, or a bit of *Jackass*, or allowing Jamie to lead us through the intricacies of a Final Fantasy game.

This openness to popular culture should not mean an abandonment of the established literature that has historically been valued in schools. Jamie was allowed to write his media-driven fantasies—and he regularly listened with his class while his teacher, Mike Anderson, read *The Lion, the Witch, and the Wardrobe*; *Tom Sawyer*; *The Giver*; and *The Hobbit*. To borrow Jamie's analogy, Anderson created a "big room," one that could admit popular culture *and* classical literature, and where children, in their writing, often merged the two in unexpected ways.

## Allow Cartooning as Serious Business

In almost any elementary classroom there is a clearly identifiable small group of boys. They seem young for their age, immature, and addicted to drawing. They will painstakingly draw their specialty—a fighter jet, a mechanical scorpion, a particularly warty goblin—again and again and again, ignoring the pleas of the teacher to get some writing done while they are at it. These boys are self-taught, and so immersed in a world of fantasy and popular culture that they are just as much of a problem to the art teacher who's pushing them to imitate high-status artists like Monet as they are to their regular classroom teacher.

Many artists and cartoonists recognize themselves in these students, and some, like Dav Pilkey and Roger Essley, have taken it upon themselves to open opportunities to such boys (and their classmates). Pilkey includes one of George and Harold's cartoons in each of his *Captain Underpants* adventures, thus providing an approachable model for visual storytelling, an earlier Dav Pilkey. Some of his Amazon.com admirers claim that they can't wait to start their own comic books.

Essley has taken this visual approach a step farther, developing what he calls a "telling board" approach where students develop a story by drawing on the storyboarding practice used by many picture-book writers and animators. Students develop stories by drawing quick rough sketches of the key action and by taping these sketches, in sequence, to a large board. In this way students and teachers can see the entire story at a glance. Like an animator presenting the idea for a cartoon, students tell their story to the class, and as a class, they discuss if there is a "hook"—a "focus or central point . . . something exciting/funny/scary" in the story. The next step is to develop the telling board into a picture book, though Essley notes it could also lead into a cartoon.

In this approach the print-based writing is built on drawing and oral storytelling, both often stronger and more appealing systems for students with learning difficulties (Essley was one himself). Essley notes that many individual education plans (IEPs) for special education students identify them as visual learners and require multimodal approaches to literacy learning—yet relatively few teachers are comfortable enough with visual storytelling to make this an option. Despite the bold promises of the IEP, special education students typically face a world of worksheets and exercises that make no use of drawing or visual abilities. Cartooning and "tellingboarding" can be the critical bridge for such students, most of them, of course, boys.

## Acknowledge the Complexity of "Violence" in Reading and Writing

In the opening scene of Martin Cruz Smith's thriller *Havana Bay* (1999), a putrefied body is being removed from the Havana harbor by a group of divers:

As the diver steadied the head, the pressure of his hands liquefied the face and made it slide like a grape skin off the skull, which itself separated cleanly from the neck: it was like trying to lift a man who was perversely disrobing part by part. A pelican sailed overhead, red as a flamingo.

"I think the identification is going to be more complicated than the captain imagined," Arkady said.

The diver caught the jaw as it dropped from off from the skull and juggled each, while the detectives pushed the other black, swollen limbs pell-mell into the shrivelling inner tube. (4–5)

This is graphic violence, realism meant to shock and repel. It is what Hodge and Tripp (1986) call "high modality" violence, writing that dwells skillfully on the detailed physiological effects of death. In my experience such graphic descriptions are rare in student writing. For all the claims that males like to write about blood and gore, their writing seems sanitized and stylized ("low modality") when compared with the work of writers like Smith. The detail that he employs requires a knowledge of human biology that students lack; it probably crosses a comfort zone (recall Corey's description of the "right amount of blood"); and from the point of view of the young writer, it slows the forward movement of the plot.

The student writers I interviewed rarely even used the term "violence" at all; they claimed to like "action" and "adventure" and saw various forms of threat, contest, and combat as essential elements of what they were attempting. In most cases there was a cartoonlike, slapstick quality to these accounts. Any categorical banning of violence would effectively preclude their attempting their favorite genres, removing one of the few motivations boys have to attempt writing. At the same time, I felt that the boys I interviewed recognized that there can be some reasonable limits; in fact, I don't think *they* would endorse a situation where there were absolutely no restrictions on representations of violence. Here are some issue or claims that I have tried to make about violence in this book:

*Writing that causes teachers or classmates to feel threatened or belittled is inappropriate.* There is a distinction between writing that has a violent effect (fear of being harmed, severe embarrassment, being mocked because of racial/ethnic identity or physical appearance)—and writing that employs violence (battles, shooting, missiles) without having a negative effect on others in the class. Admittedly, this is not always an easy line to draw, but this principle might help in making distinctions. And one would hope that we can discuss this issue with students who cross the line without automatically invoking criminal penalties.

*Violence in the media—and its effect on us—should be a topic of discussion.* For me, the most interesting sections of the student interviews dealt with their theories about media violence. What is its effect upon them? What are appropriate limits? What limits would they set for their own kids? What is its role in fostering violence in our culture? What makes someone susceptible to media violence? When is violence necessary in a story? When is it too much? Why do we "enjoy" violence? Why do we "enjoy" being scared? When does a movie become "too scary?"

Even young children have opinions on these centrally important questions. In the end, discussions of these questions are more important than any rule because they suggest that the issue is complex. Violence is both abhorrent and fascinating; it is a social problem and a central element of the movies and books enjoyed by the most nonviolent among us.

*Is it violence or comedy that young writers are after (or both)?* Children's stories, as we have seen, are often rough approximations of the TV and movie narratives they enjoy. Even "low class" popular films like Jackie Chan's *Rush Hour* movies or the *Lethal Weapon* series with Mel Gibson and Danny Glover employ storytelling techniques far more sophisticated than anything young students can match. One thing they skillfully accomplish is meshing action and comedy; often the detective team is mismatched in some way—they squabble, get in each other's way, or just get on each other's nerves due to enforced proximity. This humorous action allows us to see the characters as human and subject to irritation; it lightens the drama of crime, danger, violence, and detection. This humor also has a distancing effect, marking the story as safely unrealistic, "low modality."

Even a writer like Jamie, so in love with his action plots, stops long enough for his protagonists to argue:

> "Hey, Where's Daron??" asked Matt.
>
> "I don't know and I don't care," answered Kujo.
>
> "Hey! Hello! We need Daron for the mission!" said Matt very angrily.
>
> "What ever" said Kujo.
>
> "WHAT EVER!!! We need Daron for the mission!!!!" screamed Matt.

Finally Kujo agrees to search for Daron: "OK as long as you SHUT UP!!!" In this exchange, Jamie is trying for that humorous interplay (imagine him reading aloud "Hey! Hello!") among protagonists that is characteristic of so many action adventures.

In fact, I would argue that the action writing that is most successful with peers—male and female—is that which successfully employs humor in the form of slapstick, parody, exaggeration, or comedic exchanges among main characters. Humor, not endless violent action, is the real key to popularity among young writers. These humorous interludes become anticipated moments during oral readings, and confer a status to the writer. Familiarity with their true models—the films, TV shows, and video games students are imitating—can help us at least talk with them about their attempts, using the reference points they are familiar with. But that, of course, means that we must accept these visual narratives, at least some of them, as legitimate models.

*Action writing as a channel for male activity.* Watch any first-grade boys composing and you will see the drama of hands simulating explosions, accompanied by sound effects, with intervals of consultations with friends about who is in which spaceship. Meanwhile the artist in the group is painstakingly drawing a jet fighter, with elaborate gun mounts and lines simulating the projection of missiles and demolition of targets. I realize that this is a masculine nightmare to some, an exercise in hyper–male bonding.

Yet these opportunities for action narratives often explain why writing can become so popular among boys. Literacy too often seems unappealing and inactive to boys. It gets in the way of the need to move, to talk, to play, to live in and with one's body. In one sense, reading and writing represent the choice of language over physical action, the vicarious over the actual. But writing time often provides the most open space (outside of recess) in the curriculum—a space to enact fantasies of power, adventure, and friendship. And as many boys claim, when they are writing these adventures, they feel themselves physically inside the stories. Rather than denying the physical needs of boys, writing can employ that energy—if we can keep the space open for their play.

## Accept Youth Genres

Children combine the cultural resources at their disposal to create "youth genres," which may differ in significant ways from the literature that appeals to adults. In *Emile*, Jean Jacques Rousseau made this thunderous claim about human development, which became an underlying principle in the study of children:

> Childhood has its own ways of seeing, thinking, and feeling which are proper to it. Nothing is less sensible than to want to substitute ours for theirs. ([1762] 1979, 90)

Turning children into precocious, adultlike performers, according to Rousseau, was a great perversion of the natural order—a deprivation of childhood itself.

I feel this principle was abandoned in much of the early writing process work, when the model of the adult writer was superimposed upon young writers. Adult writers revise—therefore young writers should revise. Adult writers receive editing help from peers—therefore the same should be true for young writers. Adults write memoirs—therefore young writers should want to do the same. The list could go on. At national conferences where children's writing was presented, it was common for sophisticated, adultlike narratives to be featured along with commentaries where young writers sounded wise beyond their years. No bathroom humor or intergalactic battles. Few examples of kids obsessed with funny names.

If the developmental principle is abandoned (as I think it often has been), the task of teaching becomes one-directional—to teach the craft of practicing writers. We teach about leads and detail, conflict, setting, and other craft issues. But researchers like Dyson complicate this picture by suggesting that children often employ *their* cultural materials toward *their* ends, which may differ in significant ways from the ways adults work. John Updike does not use his fiction to directly celebrate his friendship with Anne Tyler (of course asking her permission in advance to be in his stories). But children's stories often perform this "social work" even when the persistent naming of friends may seem to us superfluous.

We might summarize some of the features of these "youth genres," particularly the work of boys, as follows:

● Fiction becomes a way of assuming freedoms, powers, and competencies that the writer does not possess in real life. It is an act of wish fulfillment, not an accurate and realistic rendering of their actual, constrained experiences.

● The pace of narrative is quick. If there *is* reflection, it has to do with how protagonists can handle a situation, not how an experience has affected them. The writing seems more cinematic than literary, with the pace of an action movie or cartoon.

● The writing works to celebrate and solidify friendship groups. Friends are mentioned by name, often like a roster of *dramatis personae*, at the beginning of a story. By employing shared loyalties to sports teams and popular youth culture

("He's back!"), young writers also affirm their existence as a group, separate from adults. As we will see in "The Dead Cashier," exerpted below, this "social work" can also involve cross-gender teasing.

● The writing often moves to the exaggerated, extreme, and absurd; the slapstick; even the silly. Any mention of the bathroom, underwear, or throwing up is good for a laugh. Sound effects, another cinematic borrowing, are also more important than they would be for adults.

"The Dead Cashier" was written by Jessica, a fourth-grade girl, who found it so funny that she could barely contain her own giggling when she read it to me. Dedicated to "the cashiers that work at Market Basket" (a local supermarket chain), it combines elements of a conventional girl friendship story and an over-the-top monster story involving two of the more popular boys in the class, one of whom is chased through the store. The story mixes traditionally male and female story types in an ingenious way.

It opens with Andrea at her friend Jessica's house on shopping day. They look for ice cream, but the container is empty. After that they play Diddy Kong Racing on Nintendo 64 and watch TV. A commercial comes on:

> It was about BEHOLD THE POWER OF CHEESE, and it showed the moon made out of cheese. Andrea and Jessica said to themselves, "What is the big whoop about cheese? It's just cheese."

But the commercial makes them hungry for soup, which is also unavailable and on the shopping list. Thus the table is set for the food-store adventure. Jessica and Andrea drop out of the story and Jake and Ethan, who are buying Cocoa Flakes, become the characters who must confront the "dead cashier."

> The cashier that Jake and Ethan were at looked a little weird. He had a nose ring like a bull, horns sticking out of his head, his finger-

nails were an inch long, warts on his hands, bolts sticking out of his shoulders, neck, and head, he had bloody wounds all over, he had blood dripping fangs like a vampire, he had tan wet skin, he had wrinkly flesh and finally he had red eyes.

After scanning the third item, the cashier begins to chase Jake, who tries to escape into the girls' bathroom—only to find "the cashier sitting on a toilet." The escape becomes a slapstick demolition of the store:

> When [Jake] was running he bumped into a box of bananas. The box of bananas tumbled down. Jake ran and the bananas fell on top of the cashier and then he slipped on a banana, slid, and bumped into a box of watermelons. The watermelons tumbled over him and one landed on his stomach but he managed to get up.

At one point in the chase, the "dead cashier" bends over, cracks his back, and seems to be truly dead. Jake falls for the act:

> Then Jake walked over to the DEAD cashier and when Jake went up to take a close look at the cashier his eyes opened quickly and [he] got up like a bolt of lightening.

Finally, cornered in an aisle, Jake is captured and eaten—"The only thing left of him was his world series baseball cap."

Jessica's story is a fine example of what Anne Dyson calls a "hybrid text," one in which there is an "intermingling [of] voices drenched in cultural meaning" (1993, 211). Jessica combines the realistic domestic world, involving her mother and best friend, with the cartoonlike fantasy of a monstrous cashier (and the opportunity for "gross" writing). Into that imagined fantasy she places two of the most popular boys in the class; so even this fantasy accomplishes the social work of cross-gender teasing. This mockery involves bathroom humor, the automatically funny intrusion of a boy into the girls' bathroom. And, throughout, there is a precise naming of consumer culture products. Dyson would refer to these strands as the intermingled "multiple worlds" of the

writer; Jessica's story is multifunctional, maintaining and affirming relationships with particular friends (male and female), amus-
ing the class, and doing "schoolwork" all at the same time. One
cannot simply place this story on a grid of realistic fiction, pushing the writer to develop her characters more carefully—that
would entirely miss the intent of her writing.

In responding to many of these stories, teachers need to enter
into the fantasy and play of creation—to join the game. This was
the case with a story written by third grader Barry in a double class
taught by David McCormick and Ann Pinto, both known for their
senses of humor. Barry's story involved the eating rampage of two
characters, Bigfoot and Monstermouse. There is a battle at the
Empire State Building, after which the monsters come to their
school, where they eat eleven teachers and 272 kids for lunch.
David's response was to make a list of the eleven teachers probably eaten—he and Ann weren't, of course, on the list. This led to
a revision, the only one I could see, where Barry changed the
eleven to twelve teachers, and "Mr. McCormick got gulped down
like a pill."

Barry inspired Joe, a classmate, to write a story where he has
a dream that he's a werewolf going on a similar eating rampage,
but when he wakes up, the "weird thing was I was stuffed full."
Ms. Pinto is eaten and described as "sour as an apple." I asked
what her reaction was:

> She's like, "Oh that's inspiring. Better put Mr. McCormick
> in." And I'm like, "I did." And she's like, "Good."

I don't think either Ann or David even thought about these reactions as teaching responses; it was surely their instinctive love of
play and teasing at work. But their reaction did open space for
more writing, for revision, and even for these coded expressions
of affection. No response rubric, outlining the "official" qualities
of good writing, can guide such intuitive teaching.

## Make Room for Obsession

Some degree of obsessiveness, even narrowness, is essential for literacy development. The noted art educator Eliot Eisner once told a group of teachers that he had no use for "well-rounded" students because "they could roll in any direction." He was making the case for what he called "productive idiosyncracies," quirky obsessions and abilities that the unrounded students (like Jamie) bring to school. Yet there is an iron law of curriculum development that often makes little room for these narrowly focused students who return again and again to an intensely imagined world. Conventional curricula focus on breadth, on lists (usually long lists) of objectives, which allow little time for extended engagement and reengagement with the same story types, certainly not for Jamie's small epics. Readers who fixate on one author or series (The Babysitter's Club, Stephen King, Dav Pilkey) are often nudged to diversify their reading—even though I have found that active adult readers frequently point to these obsessive, "narrow" periods as crucial to their development (recall Andrew Schneller with his lasers, underwater troopers, and sharks).

Standard curricula (and the more recent state frameworks) typically focus on coverage to the extent that one wonders how sustained, self-chosen writing can survive at all amid the various objectives. Here, for example, is *one* of the social studies standards in New Hampshire:

> Demonstrate a basic understanding of the origin, development, and distinctive characteristics of major ancient, classical, and agrarian civilizations including Mesopotamian, Ancient Hebrew, Egyptian, Nubian (Kush), Greek, Roman, Gupta Indian, Han Chinese, Islamic, Byzantine, Olmec, Mayan, Aztec, and Incan civilizations. (New Hampshire State Frameworks, Social Studies, Standard 18)

This standard, according to the frameworks, should be accomplished *by the end of sixth grade*. Which only goes to prove a point made by the educational reformer Alfie Kohn—the standards movement is going to make satire obsolete.

The central characteristic of an obsession is repetition that to the outsider seems extreme, even nonproductive. The obsessive student seems to persist in an activity beyond the point of mastery, and we regularly talk about the student being "in a rut." Andrew Schneller talked about persisting in his "sharks and lasers" theme for years, as does Jamie with his media-inspired adventures (he would even pick up a narrative he started years before). In many cases teachers do not share any affection for the models (e.g., action cartoons) these students are working from, so it is hard to imagine the pleasure of the genre itself, let alone the pleasure of repeating a story type dozens of times. The narrow innovations in each reiteration seem inadequate evidence of reasonable "growth."

But let me make a few points in defense of these obsessive writers.

⬧ Obsessive writers rarely create exact reproductions of the visual models they enjoy—they are transforming them (not always drastically, to be sure) and mixing them with other cultural "worlds," often involving their friends. Here for example is one fifth grader telling how he altered a TV show, *The Haunted Mask* (he refers to it as the "real" story):

> In the real story they go into a costume shop [to get the mask]. In this they get it in an alley from a man. And it doesn't start to rain. They just venture into a mansion. Anyway, it rains in this story and it doesn't rain in the real version. And in the real version they don't go into a mansion they go into an old, old shack or something. And in this they go into a mansion. And they don't meet a rock star who is really crazy in the mansion, they meet this old man that's a nut. And in

my story at the end they go to the police and in this
story the police check it out and in that story no one
checks it out.

In other words, the writer takes the original story and impro-
vises, most notably by substituting a fairly creepy rock star,
Marilyn Manson, for the old man in the "real" story.

● Similarly, they are rarely exactly repeating themselves,
although the innovations may not always seem significant to
the adult reader (e.g., the introduction of a new, more powerful weapon). Still it is important to track these innovations, to
enter into the problem solving an invention of the writer. The
more the teacher knows about the sources of the writing, the
more he or she can enter into the creation.

● Finally, what seems like excessive repetition to the outsider
does not feel that way to the child absorbed in Gundam Wing,
or The Babysitters Club, or the Dallas Cowboys. One of my
strongest impressions of reading and playing with my own
children was their immense capacity for repetition. I would
play peekaboo with Sarah at one year, and it was a charming
game the first couple of dozen times, but that wouldn't be
enough. My kids wore me down every time. They would want
books reread so many times that I had to throw in improvisa-
tions and silliness to keep *my* interest. I was frankly sick of
Richard Scarry's Lowly Worm in those busy picture books.

Learning outside of school often has a different rhythm than
learning inside. Understandably, school curricula seem to foster a
"master-and-move-on" pace; to dwell on a "mastered" skill is to
waste time and avoid the challenge of skill development. It is to
stay on one "level," to stagnate. This is an almost muscular view
of literacy development, as if the reader/writer is continually plac-
ing another weight on the exercise machine, continually moving
up a color on the old SRA.

This view, it seems to me, must be balanced by an acknowledgment of the value of persistence with genre and authors, even when the tasks children choose for themselves seem familiar or repetitive. It is as if they are working with old friends, improvising within well-known story types. Every Babysitters Club book is somewhat different, yet there is comfort knowing the general formula of the book. Jamie will employ his mechanical scorpion in most of his narratives, but not always in the same way or with the same results. I wonder, after all, how many adult readers constantly "challenge" themselves, rather than choosing to reenter the fictional worlds of well-known writers.

## Resist Narrowness

We must resist those forces that would narrow the range of writing (and reading) allowable in schools. Such restriction will invariably most hurt students outside the mainstream, those who draw their inspiration from low-status cultural sources. The "reform" movement at work in U. S. schools clearly sees standardization and uniformity as central to the goal of "not leaving any child behind." If schools clearly define objectives and test for those objectives, the energy of education can be profitably focused and performances of schools can be tracked. Where previously marginalized students were allowed to drift from grade to grade without acquiring basic skills, now schools will be accountable, and, if they don't produce, be identified as "failing schools" and presumably shamed or threatened into self-improvement. Reformers piously claim that they are not determining teaching strategies, only the objectives—yet if objectives are minutely described (and if tests are high-stakes), they invariably morph into classroom practices.

Writing instruction comes to resemble test taking—a prompt-and-rubric approach, tightly timed and lacking in any social interaction. These rubrics predetermine the qualities of successful writing, and are not likely to include the traits that make writing appealing to children. I've never seen "silly names" as a key trait, nor the capacity to create frightening technological monsters, nor the imaginative involvement of friends. Anne Dyson claims that this narrow instructional focus fails to engage the social and cultural resources (and energies) of children: "Tightly structured tasks and interactive spaces do not ensure tightly focused children—but they may make substantive interplay between social worlds problematic"(1993, 187).

The reliance on rubrics also can short-circuit the task of response, to the point where it seems that no human response is going on at all. I offer as an example the case of a Los Angeles kindergarten class where the teacher was training students to get the highest rating for their drawings. To avoid charges of exaggeration I will quote in full the description, which was offered as an exemplary practice by *Educational Leadership* magazine:

> A kindergarten teacher shared with other teachers the value and impact that scoring guides had on her children. In class, the teacher held up a drawing of a scene outside the classroom and explained to the kindergartners what parts of the drawing gave a clear picture of the environment outside the school. She explained what elements the students needed to include in their drawing to receive the highest score of 4.
>
> "Notice how the drawing shows the ground colored green and brown," she said. "There is also a tree, the sky, some clouds, and the sun."When she held up a second drawing, she explained how it was similar to the first but the tree, the clouds, and the sun weren't as clearly defined. That was why the drawing received a 3.
>
> As she discussed the next two drawings, the children started to point out what was missing and noted that they deserved a score of 2 or 1. Then the teacher instructed the children to do two things: first to create artwork that met the requirements of the level 4 drawing and second, to ask another student to evaluate the work and agree on which of the four posted samples the drawing most resembled. (Berman, Cross, and Evans 2000, 39–40)

It is difficult to imagine a more developmentally inappropriate task—who has the heart to mess with kindergartners' drawings? The approach predetermines what these kindergartners *will notice* when they look out the window (Do all kids notice the clouds? Can they even see the sun when they look out a window?). At an age where the children's art is wonderfully idiosyncratic, this "instruction" pushes them all into a conventionalized, schematic pattern. Yet if raising scores keeps a school from being designated as failing, we can surely expect to see more of the same.

In one of my interviews, a bright fourth-grade boy explained that in a "quest story" there is a need for some event to precipitate the journey of the main character, who is transformed by what he experiences. As I think about it, the account you have just read is a sort of quest, precipitated by horrific events in our schools and the anxiety about boys that they precipitated. I am, of course, not the main character, more often just a middle-aged man with a tape recorder, looking for quiet rooms in crowded schools. But it *has* been a journey into a wild fictionland—where humor and horror intertwine, where friends and rock stars interact, and where, like a good movie, there is always the possibility of a sequel. These stories defy the conventions of good realistic fiction, representing instead a utopian space that, if we believe their accounts, the kids enter bodily, and where they can enact fantasies in which they are braver and more powerful than they are in the confined spaces of home and school.

At times in the interviews I could even watch this inventive power at work. The following exchange was triggered by a report on Uranus that contained the line "Its nature remained a mystery." I asked Karen what part she liked and she mentioned this line. I asked her why:

KAREN: I just think about Star Wars and Luke Skywalker and Hans Solo battling against Darth Vader and that tune that goes "do,do,do,do/do,do,do,do"—like an unknown thing.

**TN:** When you [Liz] wrote this did you imagine you were there?

**LIZ** (*Immediately*): Yeah, I kind of pictured I was there exploring a planet or something.

**TN:** And when you thought you were there, what did you think was most important for you?

**LIZ:** Like how fast the wind went and you could go off the edge of the planet.

**TN:** Off the edge of the planet?

**LIZ** (*Laughs*): Yeah. I mean if you just kept walking, would you fall off or stay there?

Conversations like this one, where fact and fiction play off each other, are evidence of the "age of romance" that Alfred North Whitehead claimed was the characteristic of this age:

> Ideas, facts, relationships, stories, histories, possibilities, artistry in words, in sounds, in form and color crowd into a child's life, stir the feelings, excite the appreciation, and incite his impulses to kindred activity. (1967, 21)

In this case the topic of space and the single word *mystery* were potent enough to set off a chain of associations and connections to popular culture.

Whitehead calls this stage of development a time of "ferment"—which we can see in the work of Sam, a third grader, and his friends, who are part way through an epic, fourteen-book series of Alien books. Here are the completed and proposed chapters:

Book 1: There's an Adventure in a Closet (Sam)
Book 2: The Adventures of Wacky the Alien (Andrew)
Book 3: Do-Do Goes Crazy (Sam)
Book 4: Do-Do's Trip to New York (Sam)
Book 5: The Trip to Uranus (Andrew)
Book 6: Do-Do's Monopoly Mania (Sam)
Book 7: Muscleman Plays Hockey (Dan)
Book 8: Heartbreaker Falls in Love (Connor)

Book 9: Crazzzy Plays for the Pluto Isolaters (Connor)
Book 10: Heartbreaker's Divorce (Connor)
Book 11: Heartbreaker Becomes a Goalie (Connor)
Book 12: Muscleman Goes Crazy (Dan)
Book 13: Crazzzy Goes Coo-Coo (Chris)
Book 14: Do-Do's Birthday (Sam)

They included a page with the drawings of the major characters of the series, twenty in all. In one of the completed books, *Do-Do Goes Crazy*, Do-Do is in a hospital to have a broken leg treated, and, seeing a patient playing SuperMario, he jumps into the game and begins wandering in the game. Seeing a winter picture within the game, he jumps in that (so he is now two levels into the screen) and begins skiing down a hill. He is thrown out of this first level and runs into Mario himself, and they begin shouting at each other:

> Mario said, "It'sa me, Mario." Do-do said, "But it'sa me, Mario." Mario said, "No it'sa me, Mario." Do-do said, "IT'SA me, MARIO!!!!" Mario screamed, "IT'SA ME, MARIO." He was so mad he kicked Do-Do out of the screen.

Sam picked out this part of the story as his favorite, and he and his partner, Danny, enjoyed repeating this line from the SuperMario cartoon.

As I spent time with young writers like Sam I came to appreciate, even marvel at, their efforts; you might say I entered their screen. They combined so much: art, video culture, friendship groups, humor, love of sports, and even a reference to Uranus, which they had studied in science. No third-grade teacher could assign, maybe even contemplate, a writing project so extensive and complex. What made it possible and appealing for Sam was the opportunity to bring together so many affiliations; or, to use Jamie's analogy, he could build an almost infinitely big room.

I'd like to give the last word to Quintilian, legendary Roman writing teacher, advisor to emperors and tutor to some of the greatest Latin writers. In this passage he describes the way he approached the younger writers under his care—and, as usual, he gets it right:

> Let that age be daring, invent much and delight in what it invents, though it be often not sufficiently severe and correct. The remedy for exuberance is easy: barrenness is incurable by any labor. That temper in boys will afford me little hope in which mental effort is prematurely restrained by judgment. I like what is produced to be extremely copious, profuse beyond the limits of propriety. (Quintilian, *Institutes*, IV, 7, p. 303, in Bizzell and Herzberg 1990)

Yes, "beyond the limits of propriety."

# REFERENCES

ABEL, DAVID. 2000. "Male Call on Campus." *Boston Globe*, 15 November, sec. A1, p. 25.

AMERICAN ASSOCIATION OF UNIVERSITY WOMEN (AAUW). 1991. *Shortchanging Girls, Shortchanging America*. Washington, DC: American Association of University Women.

————. 1992. *How Schools Shortchange Girls*. Washington, DC: American Association of University Women.

————. 1998. *Gender Gaps: Where Schools Still Fail Our Children*. Washington, DC: American Association of University Women.

*American Pie*. 1999. Chris Weitz and Paul Weitz, directors, Universal.

AMYOT, JAMES. [1572] 1941. "To the Reader." In *The Lives of Noble Greeks and Romans* by Plutarch. New York: Heritage Press.

*Anaconda*. 1997. Luis Llosa, director, Columbia Tristar.

ANDERSON, MIKE. 2000. "Violence in Boys' Writing." Paper presented at the annual conference of the National Council of Teachers of English, November, Milwaukee, WI.

ARIES, PHILIPPE. [1962] 1998. "From Immodesty to Innocence." In *The Children's Culture Reader*, edited by Henry Jenkins and translated by Robert Baldick, 41–57. New York: New York University Press.

ARISTOTLE. 1987. *The Poetics of Aristotle: Translation and Commentary*. Translated by Stephen Halliwell. Chapel Hill: University of North Carolina Press.

*Austin Powers: The Spy Who Shagged Me*. 1999. Jay Roach, director, Warner.

BARRS, MYRA. 2000. "Gendered Literacy?" *Language Arts* 77, 4 (March): 287–93.

BASE, GRAEME. 1993. *The Eleventh Hour: A Curious Mystery*. New York: Abrams.

BEISEL, NICOLA. 1997. *Imperiled Innocents: Anthony Comstock and Family Reproduction in Victorian America*. Princeton, NJ: Princeton University Press.

BELENKY, MARY, et al. 1986. *Women's Ways of Knowing: The Development of Self, Voice, and Mind*. New York: Basic Books.

BELLOW, SAUL. 1960. *The Adventures of Augie March*. New York: Vintage.

*Beowulf*. 1968. Translated by Kevin Crossley-Holland. New York: Farrar, Straus & Giroux.

BERMAN, ILENE M., CHRISTOPHER T. CROSS, and JOAN EVANS. 2000. "Results Count in Los Angeles." *Educational Leadership* 57 (5): 38–42.

BERNSTEIN, BASIL. 1966. "A Critique of the Concept of 'Compensatory Education.'" In *Education for Democracy*, edited by David Rubinstein and Colin Stoneman. Harmondsworth, England: Penguin.

BETTELHEIM, BRUNO. 1989. *The Uses of Enchantment: The Meaning and Importance of Fairy Tales*. New York: Vintage.

BIRKERTS, SVEN. 1994. *The Gutenberg Elegies: The Fate of Reading in an Electronic Age*. New York: Fawcett Columbine.

BOURDIEU, PIERRE. 1984. *Distinction: A Social Critique of the Judgement of Taste*. Translated by Richard Nice. Cambridge, MA: Harvard University Press.

BOYATZIS, CHRIS J., And GINA M. MATILLO. 1995. "Effects of 'The Mighty Morphin Power Rangers' on Children's Aggression with Peers." *Child Study Journal* 25 (4): 45–57.

BRITTON, JAMES. 1970. *Language and Learning*. Harmondsworth, England: Penguin.

BRITTON, JAMES, et al. 1976. *The Development of Writing Abilities 11–18*. London: Macmillan.

BROOKS, DAVID. 2001. "The Organization Kid." *Atlantic Monthly* 287, 4 (April): 40–55.

BUCKINGHAM, DAVID. 1993. *Children Talking Television: The Making of Television Literacy*. London: Falmer Press.

———. 1996. *Moving Images: Understanding Children's Emotional Response to Television*. Manchester, England: Manchester University Press.

BURGE, KATHLEEN. 2000. "SJC Weighing Student Rights." *Boston Globe*, 28 November, sec. B1.

CALKINS, LUCY. 1983. *Lessons from a Child: On the Teaching and Learning of Writing*. Portsmouth, NH: Heinemann.

CALKINS, LUCY, with SHELLEY HARWAYNE. 1991. *Living Between the Lines*. Portsmouth, NH: Heinemann.

CALLAHAN, RAYMOND. 1962. *Education and the Cult of Efficiency*. Chicago: University of Chicago Press.

CAMPBELL, JAY R., KRISTIN E. UBELKI, and PATRICK L. DONOHUE. 1997. *NAEP 1996 Trends in Academic Progress*. Report in Brief. Washington, DC: National Center for Educational Statistics.

*Can Do Better: Raising Boys' Achievement in English*. 1999. London: Qualifications and Curriculum Authority Publications.

CARROLL, JAMES. 2001. "Books Make Us Free and Also Human." *Boston Globe*, 19 July, op-ed page.

CARTER, REBECCA S., and ROGER A. WOJTKIEWICZ. 2000. "Parental Involvement with Adolescent Education: Do Daughters or Sons Get More Help?" *Adolescence* 35 (137): 29–45.

CHABON, MICHAEL. 2000. *The Amazing Adventures of Kavalier and Clay*. New York: Picador.

*Child's Play 2*. 1990. John Lafia, director, Universal.

CLEARY, BEVERLY. 1991. *Runaway Ralph*. New York: Avon.

*Clueless*. 1995. Amy Heckerling, director, Paramount Pictures.

COLE, NANCY. 1997. *The ETS Gender Study: How Males and Females Perform in Educational Settings*. Princeton, NJ: Educational Testing Service.

COMAN, CAROLYN. 1997. *What Jamie Saw*. New York: Puffin.

CSIKSZENTMIHALYI, MIHALY. 1990. *Flow: The Psychology of Optimal Experience*. New York: HarperCollins.

CUMMINGS, REBECCA. 1994. "Eleventh Graders View Gender Differences in Reading and Math." *Journal of Reading* 38 (3): 196–99.

DAHL, ROALD. 1998. *The BFG*. London: Puffin.

DANIELS, LEE. 1991. *Marvel: Five Fabulous Decades of the World's Greatest Comics*. New York: Abrams.

DELPIT, LISA. 1988. "The Silenced Dialogue: Power and Pedagogy in Educating Other People's Children." *Harvard Educational Review* 58 (3): 280–98.

DENBY, DAVID. 1999a. Review of *The Spy Who Shagged Me*. *New Yorker*, 5 July, 89.

———. 1999b. "Tough Cases: The Unsettling Power of *Affliction* and *A Civil Action*." *New Yorker*, 11 January, 94–95.

DEWEY, JOHN. [1900] 1956. *The Child and the Curriculum* and *The School and Society*. Chicago: University of Chicago Press.

DYSON, ANNE HAAS. 1993. *Social Worlds of Children Learning to Write in an Urban Primary School*. New York: Teachers College Press.

————. 1997. *Writing Superheroes: Contemporary Childhood, Popular Culture, and Classroom Literacy*. New York: Teachers College Press.

————. 1999. "Coach Bombay's Kids Learn to Write: Children's Appropriation of Media Material for School Literacy." *Research in the Teaching of English* 33: 367–401.

ELBOW, PETER. 1973. *Writing Without Teachers*. New York: Oxford University Press.

ELKIND, DAVID. 1981. *The Hurried Child: Growing Up Too Fast, Too Soon*. Reading, MA: Addison-Wesley.

FERGUSON, ANN ARNETT. 2000. *Bad Boys: Public Schools and the Making of Black Masculinity*. Ann Arbor: University of Michigan Press.

FESHBACH, S. 1961. "The Stimulating Versus Cathartic Effects of a Vicarious Aggressive Activity." *Journal of Abnormal and Social Psychology* 63: 181–85.

FINDERS, MARGARET. 1997. *Just Girls: Hidden Literacies and Life in Junior High*. Portsmouth, NH: Heinemann.

GALLAS, KAREN. 1998. *"Sometimes I Can Be Anything": Power, Gender, and Identity in a Primary Classroom*. New York: Teachers College Press.

GANNETT, CINTHIA. 1992. *Gender and the Journal: Diaries and Academic Discourse*. Albany: State University of New York Press.

GILLIGAN, CAROL. 1982. *In a Different Voice: Psychological Theory and Women's Development*. Cambridge, MA: Harvard University Press.

GLADWELL, MALCOLM. 2000. *The Tipping Point: How Little Things Can Make a Big Difference*. Boston: Little, Brown.

GOFFMAN, ERVING. 1959. *The Presentation of Self in Everyday Life*. New York: Anchor.

————. 1961. *Asylums: Essays on Social Situations of Mental Patients and Other Inmates*. New York: Anchor.

GRAVES, DONALD. 1983. *Writing: Teachers and Children at Work*. Portsmouth, NH: Heinemann.

————. 1989. *Experiment with Fiction*. Portsmouth, NH: Heinemann.

GRAY-SCHLEGEL, MARY ANN, and THOMAS GRAY-SCHLEGEL. 1995–1996. "The Investigation of Gender Stereotypes as Revealed Through Children's Creative Writing." *Reading Research and Instruction* 35 (2): 160–70.

GREENWALD, ELISSA A., et al. 1999. *Writing Report Card for the Nation and the States*. Washington, DC: National Assessment of Educational Progress.

HACKER, ANDREW. 2000. "The Case Against Kids." *New York Review of Books*, 30 November.

HEATH, SHIRLEY BRICE. 1983. *Ways with Words: Language, Life, and Work in Communities and Classrooms*. New York: Cambridge University Press.

HERSCH, PATRICIA. 1999. *A Tribe Apart: A Journey to the Heart of American Adolescence*. New York: Ballantine.

HICKS, DEBORAH. 2001. "Literacies and Masculinities in the Life of Young Working-Class Boys." *Language Arts* 78 (January): 217–26.

———. 2002. *Reading Lives: Working-Class Children and Literacy Learning*. New York: Teachers College Press.

HODGE, RICHARD, and DAVID TRIPP. 1986. *Children and Television: A Semiotic Approach*. Stanford, CA: Stanford University Press.

HOGGART, RICHARD. 1957. *The Uses of Literacy*. Harmondsworth, England: Penguin.

HULL, GLYNDA, et al. 1999. "Remediation as a Social Construct: Perspectives from an Analysis of Classroom Discourse." In *The Braddock Essays*, edited by Lisa Ede, 284–311. Boston: Bedford/St. Martin's.

JAMSEN, KIRSTEN. 2001. "Men Don't Go to See Their Doctors Either: Looking at the Gap Through Some Theories About Gender." Paper delivered at the annual College Composition and Communication conference, April, Minneapolis, MN.

JENKINS, HENRY. 1998. "Introduction: Childhood Innocence and Other Modern Myths." In *The Children's Culture Reader*, edited by Henry Jenkins, 1–37. New York: New York University Press.

JUDD, CHARLES, and GEORGE BUSWELL. 1922. *Silent Reading: A Study of Various Types*. Chicago: University of Chicago Press.

KATCH, JANE. 2001. *Under Deadman's Skin: Discovering the Meaning of Children's Violent Play*. Boston: Beacon Press.

KEENE, ELLIN, and SUSAN ZIMMERMAN. 1997. *Mosaic of Thought*. Portsmouth, NH: Heinemann.

KENDRICK, MAUREEN E., and ROBERTA A. MCKAY. 2001. "Widening the Lens on the Nature of Violence in Boys' Writing: A Call for Multiple Perspectives, Positionings, Stances." Paper read at the annual meeting of the American Educational Research Association, April, Seattle, WA.

KITTREDGE, CLARE. 2001. "Some See Adolescence as the Age of Violence." *Boston Globe: New Hampshire Weekly* section, 4 March, p. 1.

KLEINBERG, HOWARD. 1999. "Movie Industry Hugs Bad Taste." *Dover, NH Foster's Daily Democrat*, 2 July, editorial page.

KUNDERA, MILAN. 1984. *The Unbearable Lightness of Being*. Translated by Michael Henry Hein. New York: Harper & Row.

LANGER, JUDITH. 1995. *Envisioning Literature: Literary Understanding and Literature Instruction*. Newark, DE: International Reading Association; New York: Teachers College Press.

LANGLAND, CONNIE. 2001. "For Teens, Columbine Is Defining Moment." *Boston Sunday Globe*, 15 April, sec. A10.

LEAVITT, ROBIN L., and MARTHA BAUMAN POWER. 1997. "Civilizing Bodies: Children in Day Care." In *Making a Place for Pleasure in Early Childhood*, edited by Joseph Tobin, 39–75. New Haven: Yale University Press.

LEMANN, NICHOLAS. 2000. "The Battle over Boys." *New Yorker* 10 July, 79–82.

LENSMIRE, TIMOTHY J. 1994. *When Children Write: Critical Revisions of the Writing Workshop*. New York: Teachers College Press.

*Lethal Weapon 4*. 1998. Richard Donner, director, Warner.

LURIE, ALISON. 1990. *Don't Tell the Grown-Ups: Subversive Children's Literature*. Boston: Little, Brown.

MCAULIFFE, S. 1993–1994. "Toward Understanding One Another: Second Graders' Use of Gendered Language and Story Types." *The Reading Teacher* 47 (4): 302–10.

MCCLAM, ERIN. 2000. "Women Widen Their Majority at Georgia Universities." *Boston Globe*, 23 August, sec. A5.

*McGuffey's Fifth Eclectic Reader*, rev. ed. 1879. New York: American Book Company.

MANGUEL, ALBERTO. 1996. *A History of Reading*. New York: Viking.

*The Mask of Zorro*. 1998. Martin Campbell, director, Columbia Tristar.

MAYHEW, KATHERINE CAMP, and ANNA CAMP EDWARDS. 1966. *The Dewey School*. New York: Atherton Press.

MECKLER, LAURA. 1999. "Drop in Teen Crime Reported." *Boston Globe*, 9 July, sec. A3.

MILLARD, ELAINE. 1997. *Differently Literate: Boys, Girls, and the Schooling of Literacy*. London: Falmer Press.

———. 2001. "Aspects of Gender: How Boys' and Girls' Experiences of Reading Shape Their Writing." In *Writing in the Elementary Classroom: A Reconsideration*, edited by Janet Evans. Portsmouth, NH: Heinemann.

MILLER, JANE. 1996. *School for Women*. London: Virago Press.

MONTAIGNE, MICHEL DE. [1595] 1987. *The Complete Essays*. Translated by M. A. Screech. London: Penguin.

MUELLER, PAM. 2001. *Lifers: Learning from At-Risk Adolescent Readers*. Portsmouth, NH: Heinemann.

MUNSCH, ROBERT. 1991. *Good Families Don't*. Illustrated by Alan Daniel. New York: Yearling.

MURRAY, DONALD. 1968. *A Writer Teaches Writing: A Practical Method of Teaching Composition*. Boston: Houghton Mifflin.

———. 1982. "Teaching the Other Self: The Writer's First Reader." In *To Compose: Teaching Writing in High School and College*, 2d ed., edited by Thomas Newkirk, 113–24. Portsmouth, NH: Heinemann.

———. 1991. *Shoptalk: Learning to Write with Writers*. Portsmouth, NH: Heinemann.

———. 2001. *My Twice-Lived Life: A Memoir*. New York: Ballantine.

NATIONAL ASSESSMENT OF EDUCATIONAL PROGRESS (NAEP). 1997. *1996 Trends in Academic Progress*. Washington, DC: National Center for Educational Statistics.

———. 2000. *Projections of Educational Statistics to 2010*. Washington, DC: National Center for Educational Statistics.

———. 2001. *Mathematics—National Achievement Levels for Males and Females, 1990–2000*. Washington, DC: National Center for Educational Statistics.

———. 2001. *1992–2000 Reading Assessment*. Washington, DC: National Center for Educational Statistics.

NEW HAMPSHIRE STATE FRAMEWORKS. Social Studies. www.ed.state.nh.us/CurriculumFrameworks/k-126.htm.

NEWKIRK, THOMAS. 1991. "The Middle Class and the Problem of Pleasure." In *Workshop 3*, edited by Nancie Atwell. Portsmouth, NH: Heinemann.

———. 2000. "Misreading Masculinity: Speculations on the Great Gender Gap in Writing." *Language Arts* 77 (4): 294–300.

———. 2001. "The Revolt Against Realism: The Attraction of Fiction for Young Writers." *Elementary School Journal* 100 (4): 467–77.

NICKERSON, COLIN. 2001a. "Case of Canadian Student Draws Writers' Sympathy." *Boston Sunday Globe*, 21 January, sec. A5.

———. 2001b. "Paper for School Lands Its Author in Canadian Jail." *Boston Globe*, 11 January, sec. A1.

*Nightmare on Elm Street 3*. 1987. Chuck Russell, director, New Line Studios.

Nystrand, Martin. 1997. *Opening Dialogue: Understanding the Dynamics of Language and Learning in the English Classroom.* New York: Teachers College Press.

Philips, Susan Urmston. 1983. *The Invisible Culture: Communication in Classroom and Community on the Warm Springs Indian Reservation.* New York: Longman.

Pilkey, Dav. 1997. *The Adventures of Captain Underpants.* New York: Scholastic.

———. 2000. *Captain Underpants and the Perilous Plot of Professor Poopypants.* New York: Scholastic.

Plato. [375 BCE] 1955. *The Republic.* Translated by Desmond Lee. London: Penguin Books.

Pollack, William. 1998. *Real Boys: Rescuing Our Sons from the Myths of Boyhood.* New York: Random House.

Postman, Neil. 1982. *The Disappearance of Childhood.* New York: Delacorte Press.

Pottorff, Donald D., Deborah Phelps-Zientarski, and Michele E. Skovera. 1996. "Gender Perceptions of Elementary and Middle School Students About Literacy at Home and School." *Journal of Research and Development in Education* 29 (4): 203–11.

Pratt, Mary Louise. 1996. "Arts of the Contact Zone." In *Ways of Reading,* 4th ed., edited by David Bartholomae and Anthony Petrosky. Boston: Bedford Books.

Quatman, Teri, and Cary Watson. 2001. "Gender Differences in Adolescent Self-Esteem: An Exploration of Domains." *Journal of Genetic Psychology* 162: 93–118.

Quintilian. [95] 1990. "From *Institutes of Oratory.*" In *The Rhetorical Tradition: Readings from Classical Times to the Present,* edited by Bizzell and Herzberg. Boston: Bedford Books.

Rabelais, Francois. [1534] 1946. *Histories of Gargantua and Pantagruel.* Translated by J. M. Cohen. London: Penguin.

Reese, Clyde M., et al. 1997. *NAEP 1996 Mathematics Report Card for the Nation and States, Executive Summary.* Washington, DC: National Assessment of Educational Progress.

Reynolds, David S. 1988. *Beneath the American Renaissance: The Subversive Imagination in the Age of Emerson and Melville.* New York: Knopf.

Rideout, Victoria, et al. 2000. *Kids, Media, and the New Millennium.* Menlo Park, CA: Henry J. Kaiser Foundation.

RIST, ROBERT. 1970. "Student Social Class and Teacher Expectations: The Self-Fulfilling Prophesy in Ghetto Education." *Harvard Educational Review* 40: 411–51.

ROSE, MIKE. 1989. *Lives on the Boundary: The Struggles and Achievements of America's Underprepared.* New York: Free Press.

ROSENBLATT, LOUISE. 1978. *The Reader, the Text, the Poem: The Transactional Theory of the Literary Work.* Carbondale, IL: Southern Illinois University Press.

ROSENTHAL, NADINE. 1995. *Speaking of Reading.* Portsmouth, NH: Heinemann.

ROUSSEAU, JEAN-JACQUES. [1762] 1979. *Emile or On Education.* Translated by Allan Bloom. New York: Basic Books.

*Rush Hour.* 1998. Brett Ratner, director, New Line Studio.

RUTENBERG, JIM. 2001. "Violence Finds a Niche in Children's Cartoons." *New York Times*, 28 July. Also found at www.nytimes.com/2001/01 /28/business/28TOON.html.

SABIN, ROGER. 1996. *Comics, Comix, and Graphic Novels: A History of Comic Art.* London: Phaidon.

SADKER, DAVID, and MYRA SADKER. 1995. *Failing at Fairness: How Our Schools Cheat Girls.* New York: Touchstone Books.

SALAMON, JULIE. 2001. "Teenage Viewers Declare Independence." *New York Times*, 13 March, sec. B1.

SCHNEIDER, JENIFER JASINSKY. 2001. "No Blood, Guns, or Gays Allowed! The Silencing of the Elementary Writer." *Language Arts* 78 (5): 415–25.

SHEVLOE, STEVE, and MIRIAM BAR-ON. 1995. "Media Violence." *Pediatrics* 95 (6): 949–52.

SMITH, FRANK. 1992. *Joining the Literacy Club: Further Essays into Education.* Portsmouth, NH: Heinemann.

SMITH, MARTIN CRUZ. 1999. *Havana Bay.* New York: Ballantine.

SMITH, MICHAEL D., and JEFFREY D. WILHELM. 2002. *"Reading Don't Fix No Chevys": The Role of Literacy in the Lives of Young Men.* Portsmouth, NH: Boynton Cook.

SMITHERMAN, GENEVA. 2001. *Talkin That Talk: Language, Culture, and Education in African America.* London: Routledge.

SOMMERS, CHRISTINA HOFF. 2000. *The War Against Boys: How Misguided Feminism Is Harming Our Young Men.* New York: Simon and Schuster.

STEINER, GEORGE. 1998. "Books and the End of Literature." In *Life Studies: An Analytic Reader*, 6th ed., edited by David Cavich, 274–80. Boston: Bedford Books.

THORNE, BARRIE. 1993. *Gender Play: Girls and Boys in School*. New Brunswick, NJ: Rutgers University Press.

TOBIN, JOSEPH. 2000. *"Good Guys Don't Wear Hats": Children's Talk About the Media*. New York: Teachers College Press.

TREPANIER-STREET, M., J. ROMATOWSKI, and S. MCNAIR. 1990. "Children's Responses to Stereotypical and Non-stereotypical Story Starters." *Journal of Research in Childhood Education* 5 (1): 60–72.

TWAIN, MARK [Samuel Clemens]. [1876] 1974. *The Adventures of Tom Sawyer*. New York: Grosset and Dunlap.

*U. S. News and World Report*. 2002. College rankings. www.usnews.com /college/rankings/rankindex.htm.

VINZ, RUTH. 1996. "Horrorscapes: (In)forming Adolescent Identity and Desire." *Journal of Curriculum Theorizing* 12 (4): 14–25.

VYGOTSKY, LEV. 1978. *Mind in Society* Cambridge, MA: Harvard University Press.

WERTHAM, FREDERIC. 1953. *Seduction of the Innocent*. New York: Rinehart.
———. [1953] 1998. "Such Trivia as Comic Books." In *The Children's Cultural Reader*, edited by Henry Jenkins. New York: New York University Press.

WHITEHEAD, ALFRED NORTH. [1929] 1967. *The Aims of Education and Other Essays*. New York: Free Press.

WILHELM, JEFFREY D. 1997. *"You Gotta Be the Book": Teaching Engaged and Reflective Reading with Adolescents*. New York: Teachers College Press.

WILLIAMS, BRONWYN. 2002. *Tuned In: Television and the Teaching of Writing*. Portsmouth, NH: Boynton Cook.